ESSENTIAL CROCHET

NEXT LEVEL STITCHES

PORTABLE STITCH COMPANION
Textures, Colorwork, and
Fancy Edgings

MELISSA LEAPMAN

QUARRY

Quarto.com

© 2025 Quarto Publishing Group USA Inc.
Designs © 2016 Melissa Leapman

First Published in 2025 by Quarry Books, an imprint of The Quarto Group,
100 Cummings Center, Suite 265-D, Beverly, MA 01915, USA.
T (978) 282-9590 F (978) 283-2742

Quarry Books titles are also available at discount for retail, wholesale, promotional,
and bulk purchase. For details, contact the Special Sales Manager by email at
specialsales@quarto.com or by mail at The Quarto Group, Attn: Special Sales Manager,
100 Cummings Center, Suite 265-D, Beverly, MA 01915, USA.

10 9 8 7 6 5 4 3 2 1

ISBN: 978-0-7603-9234-8

Digital edition published in 2025
eISBN: 978-0-7603-9235-5

The content in this book was previously published in *Melissa Leapman's Indispensable
Stitch Collection for Crocheters* (Creative Publishing International 2016) by Melissa Leapman.

Library of Congress Cataloging-in-Publication Data can be found under *Melissa Leapman's
Indispensable Stitch Collection for Crocheters* (Creative Publishing International 2016) by
Melissa Leapman.

Design and Page Layout: Larkin Design
Photography: Glenn Scott Photography
Technical Edit and Illustrations: Karen Manthey

Printed in China

To Alex and Chris, the two most loved—
and most beautiful—boys in the world.

CONTENTS

INTRODUCTION

What's the one thing that every crochet project has in common? Each one is made using a combination of basic, easy-to-make stitches.

If you've mastered looping yarn over your hook to create a simple chain, you already possess all the skills you need to create an infinite number of beautiful textures, lace, edgings, and colorwork. This collection includes 100 of my favorite crochet stitch patterns gathered from nearly thirty years designing for the yarn and fashion industry. Some patterns are long-standing favorites, such as Edging 14 on page 102; others, like the Saxon Braid Panel on page 44 are original to this collection. Each one can be used in almost any crochet project, making it easy to put your own spin on a commercial pattern or even to design your own!

I've included instructions in both text and symbol diagram format. Many crocheters enjoy using the international symbols so they can see exactly where the stitches go, but others prefer reading patterns completely written out in text. Choose the format that makes you and your crochet hook happy.

If a stitch or technique seems unfamiliar to you, don't worry! Just look at it as an opportunity to learn something and grow. Refer to Crochet Techniques on pages 114–139 and add a new trick or two to your skill set.

I have had a blast working on this stitch collection for you. Seeing the colorful swatches scattered around the office reminds me how versatile and fun our beloved needle art of crochet is.

I look forward to seeing all the projects you make!

One, two, three . . . go!

WHAT IS A STITCH DICTIONARY?

Ask any crocheter, and you'll learn that all crocheted fabrics, even the most intricate ones, are composed of just a few basic, easy-to-learn stitches. Various combinations of chain, single crochet, half double crochet, double crochet, triple crochet, and double triple crochet stitches can form a nearly infinite number of patterns from lace to textures to complicated-looking colorwork. A stitch dictionary is a collection of these fabric designs and can be used to create beautiful and unique projects, from snuggly baby blankets to lacy cardis to warm winter hats and more. It's easy to use these stitch patterns to customize a pattern you already have or to design a new one from scratch.

HOW TO USE THIS BOOK

This book's collection is divided into three sections according to fabric type: textured patterns, colorwork patterns, and edgings.

It was a designer's dream to combine so many techniques to create a wide variety of fabrics. If a stitch or technique looks unfamiliar to you, refer to Crochet Techniques on pages 114–139.

Adding to your backpack of skills will help you grow as a crocheter, so don't let an advanced technique stop you!

READING THE PATTERNS

I've provided every pattern in this book in both words and in symbol diagrams. If you've never worked with crochet symbols, go to page 111 to see how they work. The cool thing about these diagrams is that you never have to wonder where to insert your hook—and you'll never again lose your place in a pattern! With a little practice, the symbols will make your stitching easier, quicker, and much more fun.

Each individual stitch pattern begins with the multiple of foundation chains that are needed for the pattern. Basketweave 2, for example, on page 32 requires a multiple of 8 chains. This means you should start with a chain that is divisible by 8, such as 32 or 80 or 176.

Some patterns require extra stitches in order to center the design on the fabric, such as Two-Color Sawtooth on page 87. In this case, you'd need to start with a multiple of 8 + 2 chains, so 26 chains would work perfectly (8 × 3 + 2), as would 322 (8 × 40 + 2). Obviously, the target number of chains would depend on the desired width of the fabric, adjusting as necessary to fit the multiple noted at the beginning of the pattern.

In the diagrams, the stitch multiple, also referred to as the stitch repeat, is shaded gray. In the written instructions, the repeat usually begins with an asterisk and ends with a semicolon. Repeats of rows are designated by a bracket on the side of the diagram.

You'll see that some patterns, such as Heartbeats (page 51) and Almond Ridges (page 17) have a special icon to indicate that they look great on both sides, making them perfect for blankets, scarves and other projects for which there is no real public and private side of the fabric. Often the front and back look nearly identical. Occasionally, though, they are quite different from each other, and in these cases, photos show what both sides looks like. Who knows: You might prefer the wrong side over the right side of the fabric in some cases!

INCORPORATING THE PATTERNS IN PROJECTS

For me, the best part of being a crochet designer is playing with different combinations of stitches and finding new and interesting ways to use them as the basis for unique projects. It is my wish that you'll use the patterns in this book as a launching pad for your own fun experimentation! Here's how:

Simple Squares and Rectangles

If you're curious to try several different patterns, crochet pieces that are approximately 6" (15.2 cm) square, and in the process, you'll create an assortment of spa washcloths or useful dishcloths perfect for gift giving. (Bonus!) Or, make a giant rectangular "swatch" with finished measurements of 50" × 68" (127 × 173 cm) or 36" × 42" (91.4 × 106.7 cm) for a custom full-size throw or baby blanket, respectively. Another fun option is to sew several swatches together to create a unique sampler afghan! Just be sure every yarn in the project has the same laundering instructions. (Been there, done that!)

Swapping Stitch Patterns within Existing Patterns

If you'd like to use one of these stitch patterns in a published pattern, you simply need to ensure that your gauge matches the one originally called for. Just make a large swatch, at least 6" (15 cm) square, in the stitch pattern you'd like to use, and count the number of stitches and rows over 4 inches (10 cm). Of course, if the commercial pattern gives the gauge over 1 inch (2.5 cm) rather than 4 inches (10 cm), divide your numbers by four.

Sometimes, especially in lace and textured patterns, it is difficult to actually see—and therefore count—every stitch. To determine the gauge in these cases, measure the width of one pattern repeat and then divide by the number of stitches involved.

If the finished product will be washed and blocked, it's important to treat your gauge swatch the same way. Yarn often behaves differently after laundering: some fibers will stretch or contract lengthwise or widthwise; some might become limp while others might bloom. Use your gauge swatch as a way to test your finished fabric. It's better to make discoveries with the swatch rather than have major surprises later!

Once you finally determine that the gauge in your swatch matches the one called for in the pattern, you can easily make the substitution. You might have to adjust the number of chains in the foundation chain to accommodate the stitch multiple for your new stitch pattern.

Designing from Scratch

It's interesting to design a project from start to finish. Some of us are lucky enough to have been able to turn that process into a career!

Begin by crocheting a large gauge swatch as described at left. If you plan to use more than one stitch pattern within a single project, be sure to make separate gauge swatches for each one. Then, carefully measure your stitch and row gauges. Don't fudge during this step, since the difference of even half a stitch per inch (2.5 cm) will result in a finished project that is much larger or smaller than what was planned.

Here's the fun part: Sketch out the shape of the desired project, keeping in mind that some projects, like many garments, might be assembled from several pieces sewn together.

Then, add desired finished measurements to your drawing. You can utilize the specs from schematic drawings in published patterns as a guide—or even measure items you already own and love for a starting point.

To determine the number of stitches your piece will require, simply multiply your gauge by the desired width measurements, rounding up or down to match the stitch multiple of your stitch pattern. For example, if you'd like to crochet a 36" × 36" (91.5 × 91.5 cm) baby blanket and your measured gauge is 5 stitches to the inch (2.5 cm), you'd need 180 stitches across the width of your fabric. You might have to adjust this number slightly in order to match the stitch multiple. Designing is more of an art than a science, right?

HOW TO SHAPE PIECES WHEN WORKING PATTERN STITCHES

It's pretty straightforward to create rectangles and squares, but shaped pieces are a little more challenging.

Decreasing is achieved by working two or more stitches together; increasing is typically done by working two or more stitches where ordinarily there would only be one. For the best result, you'll want to try to maintain the original stitch pattern while shaping. To determine the most unobtrusive way to increase or decrease, draw or photocopy a large chunk of the main stitch pattern, and then pencil the shaping changes onto it.

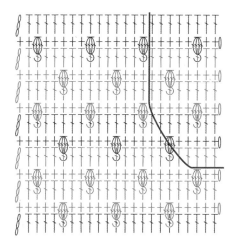

Copy and assemble a large chunk of the main pattern. Draw the shaping changes onto the pattern.

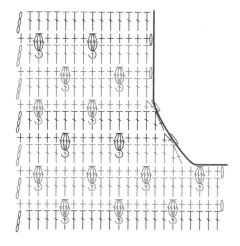

Working to match the shaping line, work decreases as needed in the appropriate stitch.

THE STITCH COLLECTION

Here's a library of crocheted stitch designs, including textured patterns, colorwork, and edgings. Most of the patterns are original to this book and are accessible and inspirational to most skill levels.

TEXTURED PATTERNS

In this section, discover how easy and fun it is to combine basic crochet stitches to create wonderfully textured fabrics. Here, post stitches, popcorns, and a few novelty maneuvers are used to stitch traditional ribbings, high-relief basketweaves, cables, and more.

RICE STITCH

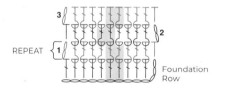

Chain a multiple of 2 + 1.

Foundation Row (RS): Dc in the fourth ch from the hook and in each ch across, turn.

Row 1 (WS): Ch 2 (counts as hdc here and throughout), skip the first st, *FPdc in the next st, BPdc in the next st; repeat from the * across, ending with FPdc in the next st, hdc in the top of the turning-ch-2, turn.

Repeat Row 1 for the pattern.

FAUX RIBBING

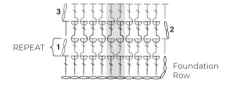

Chain a multiple of 2.

Foundation Row (RS): Dc in the fourth ch from the hook and in each ch across, turn.

Row 1: Ch 2 (counts as hdc here and throughout), skip the first hdc, *FPdc in the next st, BPdc in the next st; repeat from the * across, ending with hdc in the top of the turning-ch, turn.

Repeat Row 1 for the pattern.

HORIZONTAL CORDED

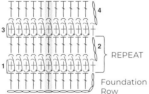

Chain any number of chains.

Foundation Row (RS): Dc in the fourth ch from the hook and in each ch across, do not turn.

Row 1 (WS): Ch 1, Working from left to right, *reverse sc (page 131) in the front loop only (page 138) of the next st; repeat from the * across, ending with a reverse sc in the top of the turning-ch-3, turn.

Row 2: Ch 3 (counts as dc here and throughout), skip the first st, *dc in the back loop only of the next dc 1 row below; repeat from the * across. Ch 1, do not turn.

Repeat Rows 1 and 2 for the pattern.

WAFFLE STITCH

Chain a multiple of 4 + 3.

Foundation Row (RS): Dc in the fourth ch from hook and in each ch across, turn.

Row 1 (WS): Ch 3 (counts as dc here and throughout), skip the first st, *FPdc in each of the next 3 dc, dc in the next dc; repeat from the * across, ending with FPdc in each of the next 3 dc, dc in the top of the turning-ch-3, turn.

Row 2: Ch 3, skip the first st, *dc in each of the next 3 sts, FPdc in the next st; repeat from the * across, ending with dc in each of the next 3 sts, dc in the top of the turning-ch-3, turn.

Repeat Rows 1 and 2 for the pattern.

GRANITE

THERMAL STITCH

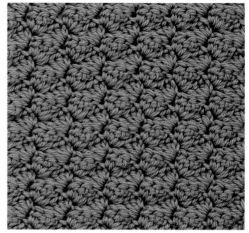

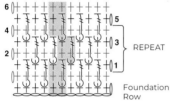

Note

Always skip the sc behind the FPtr.

Chain a multiple of 2.

Foundation Row 1 (RS): Sc in the second ch from the hook and in each ch across, turn.

Foundation Row 2: Ch 1, sc in each sc across, turn.

Row 1 (RS): Ch 1, sc in the first sc, *FPtr in the next sc 2 rows below, skip the sc after the last sc made, sc in the next sc; repeat from the * across, turn.

Row 2: As Foundation Row 2, turn.

Row 3: Sc in each of the first 2 sc, *FPtr in the next sc 2 rows below, skip the sc after the last sc made, sc in the next st; repeat from the * across, ending with sc in the last sc, turn.

Row 4: As Row 2.

Repeat Rows 1-4 for the pattern.

Chain a multiple of 4 + 2.

Foundation Row (RS): [Sc, hdc, 2 dc] in the second ch from the hook, *skip the next 3 ch, [sc, hdc, 2 dc] in the next ch; repeat from the * across, ending with skip the next 3 ch, sc in the last ch, turn.

Row 1: Ch 1, [sc, hdc, 2 dc] in the first sc, *skip the next 3 sts, [sc, hdc, 2 dc] in the next sc; repeat from the * across, ending with skip the next 3 sts, sc in the last sc, turn.

Repeat Row 1 for the pattern.

TEXTURED LATTICE

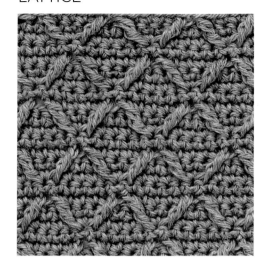

Chain a multiple of 6 + 3.

Foundation Row (RS): Sc in the second ch from the hook and in each ch across, turn.

Row 1 (WS): Ch 1, sc in each st across, turn.

Rows 2 and 3: As Row 1.

Row 4: Ch 1, sc in each of the first 3 sc, FPtr in the second sc 3 rows below, *skip the next 4 sc 3 rows below, FPtr in the next sc 3 rows below, skip the next 2 sc, sc in each of the next 4 sc, FPtr in the sc to the left of the last FPtr made 3 rows below; repeat from the * across, ending with skip the next 4 sc 3 rows below, FPtr in the next sc 3 rows below, skip the next 2 sc, sc in each of the last 3 sc, turn.

Rows 5-7: As Row 1.

Row 8: Ch 1, sc in the first sc, skip the first 4 sc 3 rows below, FPtr in the next sc 3 rows below, skip the next sc, *sc in each of the next 4 sc, FPtr in the sc to the left of the last FPtr made 3 rows below, skip the next 4 sc 3 rows below, FPtr in the next sc 3 rows below, skip the next 2 sc; repeat from the * across, ending with sc in each of the next 4 sc, FPtr in the sc to the left of the last FPtr made 3 rows below, skip the next sc, sc in the last sc, turn.

Repeat Rows 1-8 for the pattern.

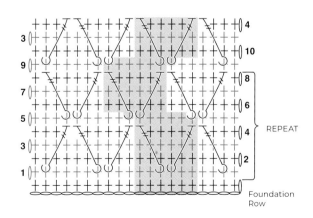

CROSS STITCH

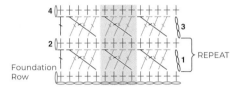

Chain a multiple of 4 + 3.

Foundation Row (WS): Sc in the second ch from the hook and in each ch across, turn.

Row 1 (RS): Ch 3 (counts as dc here and throughout), skip the first 2 sc, dc in each of the next 3 sc, working over the last 3 dc just made (enclosing them within the new stitches), dc in the last skipped sc, *skip the next sc, dc in each of the next 3 sc, working over the last 3 dc just made, dc in the last skipped sc; repeat from the * across, ending with a dc in the last sc, turn.

Row 2: Ch 1, sc in each dc across, ending with a sc in the top of the turning-ch-3, turn.

Repeat Rows 1 and 2 for the pattern.

HERRINGBONE

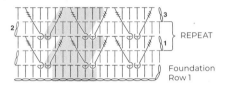

Note

Always skip the hdc behind each FPdtr.

Chain a multiple of 6 + 3.

Foundation Row 1 (RS): Hdc in the third ch from the hook and in each ch across, turn.

Foundation Row 2 (RS): Ch 2 (counts as hdc here and throughout), skip the first hdc, hdc in each hdc across, hdc in the top of the turning-ch-2, turn.

Row 1 (WS): Ch 2, skip the first 3 hdc, FPdtr in the next hdc 2 rows below, skip the hdc behind FPdtr just made, *hdc in each of the next 4 hdc, FPdtr in the hdc 2 rows below immediately to the left of the last FPdtr made, skip 4 hdc after the FPdtr just made, FPdtr in the next hdc 2 rows below, skip 2 hdc after the last hdc made; repeat from the * across, ending with hdc in each of the next 4 hdc, FPdtr in the hdc 2 rows below immediately to the left of the last FPdtr made, skip the hdc after the FPdtr just made, hdc in the top of the turning-ch-2, turn.

Row 2: Skip the first hdc, hdc in each st across, ending with hdc in the top of the turning-ch-2, turn.

Repeat Rows 1 and 2 for the pattern.

ALMOND RIDGES

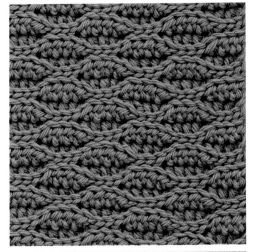

Chain a multiple of 8 + 5.

Foundation Row 1 (RS): Slip st in the second ch from the hook and in each of the next 3 ch, *hdc in each of the next 4 ch, slip st in each of the next 4 ch; repeat from the * across, turn.

Foundation Row 2: Ch 1, Working in the back loop only across the entire row (page 138), slip st in each of the first 4 slip sts, *hdc in each of the next 4 sts, slip st in each of the next 4 sts; repeat from the * across, turn.

Row 1 (RS): Ch 2 (counts as hdc here and throughout), working in the back loop only across the entire row, skip the first st, hdc in each of the next 3 sts, *slip st in each of the next 4 sts, hdc in each of the next 4 sts; repeat from the * across, turn.

Row 2: Ch 2, working in the back loop only across the entire row, skip the first st, hdc in each of the next 3 sts, *slip st in each of the next 4 sts, hdc in each of the next 4 sts; repeat from the * across, ending with slip st in each of the next 4 sts, hdc in each of the next 3 sts, hdc in the top of the turning-ch-2, turn.

Row 3: Working in the back loop only across the entire row, slip st in each of the first 4 sts, *hdc in each of the next 4 sts, slip st in each of the next 4 sts; repeat from the * across, ending with hdc in each of the next 4 sts, slip st in each of the next 3 sts, slip st in the top of the turning-ch-2, turn.

Row 4: As Foundation Row 2.

Repeat Rows 1-4 for the pattern.

Note

Work the slip stitches very loosely so it is easy to work into them on subsequent rows.

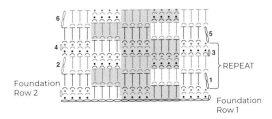

ENTWINED LATTICE

Notes

Always skip the hdc behind each FPst.

Each FPtr and FPdtr counts as a FPst.

Chain a multiple of 10 + 4.

Foundation Row 1 (RS): Hdc in the third ch from the hook and in each ch across, turn.

Foundation Row 2: Ch 2 (counts as hdc here and throughout), skip the first st, hdc in each st across, ending with hdc in top of turning-ch-2, turn.

Row 1 (RS): Ch 2, skip the first st, hdc in each of the next 3 sts *FPtr in each of the next sts 2 rows below, skip 2 sts after the last hdc made, hdc in the next st, FPtr in each of the next 2 sts 2 rows below, skip 2 sts after the last hdc made, hdc in each of the next 5 sts; repeat from the * across, ending with FPtr in each of the next sts 2 rows below, skip 2 sts after the last hdc made, hdc in the next st, FPtr in each of the next 2 sts 2 rows below, skip 2 sts after the last hdc made, hdc in each of the next 3 sts, hdc in the top of the turning-ch-2, turn.

Row 2 and all WS Rows: Ch 2, skip the first st, hdc in each st across, ending with hdc in top of turning-ch-2, turn.

Row 3: Ch 2, skip the first st, hdc in each of the next 3 sts *skip the next 3 sts, FPdtr in each of the next 2 FPsts 2 rows below, skip 2 sts after the last hdc made, hdc in the next st, working in front of the last 2 FPsts just made (page 136), FPdtr in each of the 2 skipped FPsts 2 rows below, skip 2 sts after the last hdc made, hdc in each of the next 5 sts; repeat from the * across, ending with skip the next 3 sts, FPdtr in each of the next 2 FPsts 2 rows below, skip 2 sts after the last hdc made, hdc in the next st, working in front of the last 2 FPsts just made, FPdtr in each of the 2 skipped FPsts 2 rows below, skip 2 sts after the last hdc made, hdc in each of the next 3 sts, hdc in the top of the turning-ch-2.

Row 5: Ch 2, skip the first st, hdc in the next st, *skip the next 3 sts, FPdtr in each of the next 2 FPsts 2 rows below, skip 2 sts after the last hdc made, hdc in each of the next 5 sts, FPdtr in each of the last 2 skipped FPsts 2 rows below, skip 2 sts after the last hdc made, hdc in the next st; repeat from the * across, ending with hdc in the top of the turning-ch-2, turn.

Row 7: Ch 2, skip the first st, hdc in the next st, FPtr in each of the next 2 FPsts 2 rows below, skip 2 sts after the last hdc made, *hdc in each of the next 5 sts, skip the next 3 sts, FPdtr in each of the next 2 FPsts 2 rows below, skip 2 sts after the last hdc made, hdc in the next st, working behind the last 2 FPsts just made (page 137), FPdtr in each of the 2 skipped FPsts 2 rows below, skip 2 sts after the last hdc made; repeat from the * across, ending with hdc in each of the next 5 sts, FPtr in each of the next 2 FPsts 2 rows below, skip 2 sts after the last hdc made, hdc in the next st, hdc in the top of the turning-ch-2, turn.

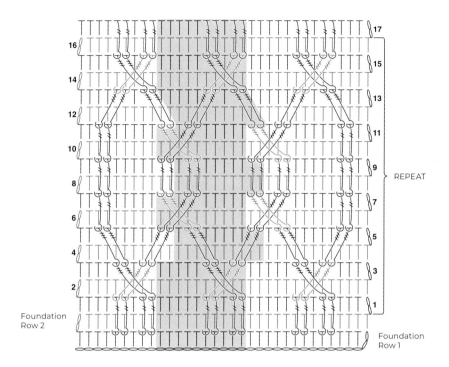

Row 9: Ch 2, skip the first st, hdc in the next st, *FPtr in each of the next 2 FPsts 2 rows below, skip 2 sts after the last hdc made, hdc in each of the next 5 sts, FPtr in each of the next 2 FPsts 2 rows below, skip 2 sts after the last hdc made, hdc in the next st; repeat from the * across, ending with hdc in the top of the turning-ch-2, turn.

Row 11: As Row 7.

Row 13: Ch 2, skip the first st, hdc in each of the next 3 sts, *FPdtr in each of the first 2 skipped FPsts 2 rows below, skip 2 sts after the last hdc made, hdc in the next st, skip the next 3 sts, FPdtr in each of the next 2

FPsts 2 rows below, skip 2 sts after the last hdc made, hdc in each of the next 5 sts; repeat from the * across, ending with FPdtr in each of the last 2 skipped FPsts 2 rows below, skip 2 sts after the last hdc made, hdc in the next st, skip the next 3 sts, FPdtr in each of the next 2 FPsts 2 rows below, skip 2 sts after the last hdc made, hdc in each of the next 3 sts, hdc in the top of the turning-ch-2, turn.

Row 15: As Row 3.

Row 16: As Row 2.

Repeat Rows 1-16 for the pattern.

SLANTED SPIKES

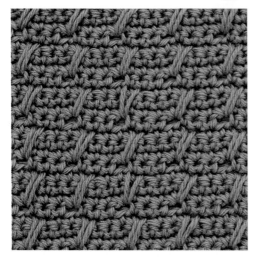

Chain a multiple of 4 + 2.

Foundation Row (RS): Sc in the second ch from the hook and in each ch across, turn.

Row 1 (WS): Ch 1, sc in the first sc, *ch 1, skip the next st, sc in each of the next 3 sts; repeat from the * across, turn.

Row 2: Ch 1, sc in each of the first 3 sts, *sc in the next ch-1 sp, sc in each of the next 3 sc; repeat from the * across, ending with sc in the ch-1 sp, sc in the last sc, turn.

Row 3: Ch 1, sc in each sc across, turn.

Row 4: Ch 1, sc in the first st, *skip the next 2 sts, elongated sc in the next ch-1 sp 3 rows below, skip the st after the last sc made, sc in each of the next 3 sts; repeat from the * across, turn.

Repeat Rows 1-4 for the pattern.

Notes

Elongated sc = Insert hook in the ch-sp 3 rows below, yarn over the hook and pull up a loop, stretching it to height required for the current Row, yarn over and draw it through both loops on the hook.

When making an elongated sc, always work over the last two rows.

Always skip the stitch behind an elongated sc.

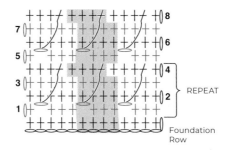

VERTICAL HONEYCOMBS

Chain a multiple of 10 + 6.

Foundation Row (RS): Dc in the fourth ch from the hook and in each ch across, turn.

Row 1 (WS): Skip the first slip st, dc in each of the next 3 sts, *skip the next st, dc in each of the next 2 sts, BPtr in the last skipped st, skip the next 2 sts, BPtr in the next st, working in front of the last BPtr made (page 136), dc in each of the 2 skipped sts, skip the st where the last BPtr was worked, dc in each of the next 4 sts; repeat from the * across, ending the row with skip the next st, dc in each of the next 2 sts, BPtr in the last skipped st, skip the next 2 sts, BPtr in the next st, working in front of the last BPtr made, dc in each of the 2 skipped sts, dc in each of the next 3 sts, dc in the third ch of the turning-ch-3, turn.

Row 2: Skip the first slip st, dc in each of the next 3 sts, *skip the next 2 sts, FPtr in the next FPtr, working behind the last FPtr made (page 137), dc in each of the skipped sts, skip the next st, dc in each of the next 2 sts, working in front of the last 2 dc made, FPtr in the last skipped FPtr, skip the st where the last FPtr was worked, dc in each of the next 4 sts; repeat from the * across, ending the row with skip the next 2 sts, FPtr in the next FPtr, working behind the last FPtr made, dc in each of the skipped sts, skip the next st, dc in each of the next 2 sts, working in front of the last 2 dc made, FPtr in the last skipped FPtr, dc in each of the next 3 sts, dc in the third ch of the turning-ch-3, turn.

Repeat Rows 1 and 2 for the pattern.

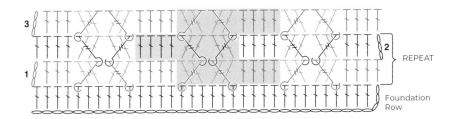

WOVEN LATTICE

Notes

Always skip the hdc behind each FPst.

Each FPtr and FPdtr counts as a FPst.

Chain a multiple of 6 + 4.

Foundation Row 1 (RS): Hdc in the third ch from the hook and in each ch across, turn.

Foundation Row 2: Ch 2 (counts as hdc here and throughout), skip the first st, hdc in each st across, ending with hdc in top of turning-ch-2, turn.

Foundation Row 3: Ch 2, skip the first st, hdc in the next st, *FPtr in each of the next 2 sts 2 rows below, skip 2 sts after the last hdc made, hdc in the next st; repeat from the

* across, ending with hdc in the top of the turning-ch-2, turn.

Foundation Row 4: As Foundation Row 2.

Row 1 (RS): Ch 2, skip the first st, hdc in the next st, *skip the next 3 sts, FPdtr in each of the next 2 FPsts 2 rows below, skip 2 sts after the last hdc made, hdc in the next st, working in front of the last 2 FPsts just made (page 132), FPdtr in each of the last 2 skipped FPsts 2 rows below, skip 2 sts after the last hdc made, hdc in the next st; repeat from the * across, ending with hdc in the top of the turning-ch-2, turn.

Row 2 and all WS Rows: Ch 2, skip the first st, hdc in each st across, ending with hdc in top of turning-ch-2, turn.

Row 3: Ch 2, skip the first st, hdc in the next st, FPtr in each of the next 2 FPsts 2 rows below, skip 2 sts after the last hdc made, hdc in the next st, *skip the next 3 sts, FPdtr in each of the next 2 sts 2 rows below, skip 2 sts after the last hdc made, hdc in the next st, working behind the last 2 FPsts just made (page 137), FPdtr in each of the last 2 skipped FPsts 2 rows below, skip 2 sts after the last hdc made, hdc in the next st; repeat from the * across, ending with FPtr in each of the next 2 FPsts 2 rows below, skip 2 sts after the last hdc made, hdc in the next st, hdc in the top of the turning-ch-2, turn.

Row 4: As Row 2.

Repeat Rows 1-4 for the pattern.

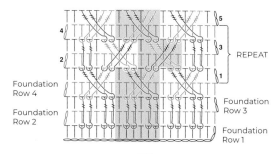

Foundation Row 4

Foundation Row 2

Foundation Row 3

Foundation Row 1

REPEAT

HONEYCOMB

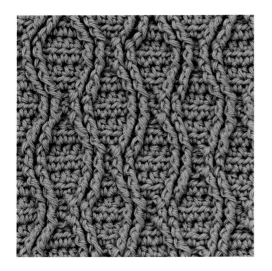

Row 1 (RS): Ch 2, skip the first hdc, FPtr in each of the next 2 sts 2 rows below, skip 2 sts after the last hdc made, *hdc in each of the next 4 hdc, FPtr in each of the next 4 sts 2 rows below, skip 4 sts after the last hdc made; repeat from the * across, ending with hdc in each of the next 4 hdc, FPtr in each of the next 2 sts 2 rows below, skip 2 hdc after the last hdc made, hdc in the top of the turning-ch-2, turn.

Row 2 and all WS Rows: Ch 2, skip the first hdc, hdc in each st across, ending with hdc in the top of the turning-ch-2, turn.

Row 3: Ch 2, skip the first hdc, hdc in each of the next 2 hdc, *FPdtr in each of the last 2 skipped FPsts 2 rows below, FPdtr in each of the next 2 FPsts 2 rows below, skip 4 hdc after the last hdc made, hdc in each of the next 4 hdc; repeat from the * across, ending with FPdtr in each of the last 2 skipped FPsts 2 rows below, FPdtr in each of the next 2 FPsts 2 rows below, skip 4 hdc after the last hdc made, hdc in each of the next 2 hdc, hdc in the top of the turning-ch-2, turn.

Row 5: Ch 2, skip the first hdc, hdc in each of the next 2 hdc, *FPtr in each of the next 4 FPsts 2 rows below, skip 4 hdc after the last hdc made, hdc in each of the next 4 hdc; repeat from the * across, ending with FPtr in each of the next 4 FPsts 2 rows below, hdc in each of the next 2 hdc, hdc in the top of the turning-ch-2, turn.

Row 7: Ch 2, skip the first hdc, *FPdtr in each of the next 2 FPsts 2 rows below, skip 2 hdc after the last hdc made, hdc in each of the next 4 hdc, FPdtr in each of the last 2 skipped FPsts 2 rows below; repeat from the * across, hdc in the top of the turning-ch-2.

Row 8: As Foundation Row 2.

Repeat Rows 1-8 for the pattern.

Notes

Always skip the hdc behind each FPst.

Each FPtr and FPdtr count as FPst.

Chain a multiple of 8 + 3.

Foundation Row 1 (RS): Hdc in the third ch from the hook and in each ch across, turn.

Foundation Row 2: Ch 2 (counts as hdc here and throughout), skip the first hdc, hdc in each st across, ending with hdc in the top of the turning-ch-2, turn.

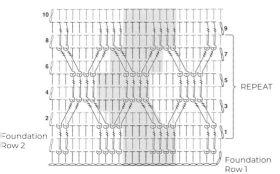

TRELLIS WITH POPCORNS PANEL

Notes

This panel is worked on a solid hdc ground.

Always skip the hdc behind each FPst.

Each FPtr, FPdc, and FPdtr counts as FPst.

Popcorn = 5 dc in the indicated st; drop the loop from the hook; reinsert the hook in the first dc of the 5-dc group, pick up the dropped loop and pull it through the first dc (page 120).

Chain 34.

Foundation Row 1 (RS): Hdc in the third ch from the hook and in each ch across, turn.

Foundation Row 2: Ch 2 (counts as hdc here and throughout), skip the first st, hdc in each st across, ending with hdc in top of turning-ch-2, turn.

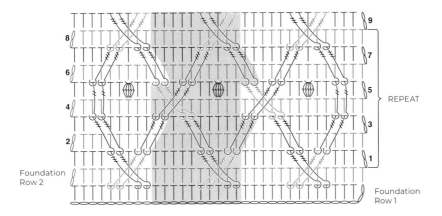

Row 1 (RS): Ch 2, skip the first st, hdc in each of the next 3 sts, skip the next 3 sts, [FPdtr in each of the next 2 sts 2 rows below, skip 2 sts after the last hdc made, hdc in the next st, working in front of the last 2 FPst just made (page 136), FPdtr in each of the first 2 skipped sts 2 rows below, skip 2 sts after the last hdc made, hdc in each of the next 5 sts] twice, skip the next 3 sts, FPdtr in the next 2 sts 2 rows below, skip 2 sts after the last hdc made, hdc in the next st, working in front of the last 2 FPsts just made, FPdtr in each of the first 2 skipped sts 2 rows below, skip 2 sts after the last hdc made, hdc in each of the next 3 sts, hdc in the top of the turning-ch-2, turn.

Row 2 and all WS Rows: Ch 2, skip the first st, hdc in each st across, ending with hdc in top of turning-ch-2, turn.

Row 3: Skip the first st, hdc in the next st, FPdtr in each of the next 2 FPsts 2 rows below, skip 2 sts after Ch 2, skip last hdc made, hdc in each of the next 5 sts, [FPdtr in each of the last 2 skipped FPsts 2 rows below, skip 2 sts after the last hdc made, hdc in the next st] 3 times, hdc in the top of the turning-ch-2, turn.

Row 5: Ch 2, skip the first st, hdc in the next st, FPtr in each of the next 2 FPsts 2 rows below, skip 2 sts after the last hdc made, hdc in each of the next 2 sts, popcorn in the next st, hdc in each of the next 2 sts, skip the next 3 sts, [FPdtr in each of the next 2 FPsts 2 rows below, skip 2 sts after the last hdc made, hdc in the next st, working behind the last 2 FPsts made (page 137), FPdtr in the 2 skipped FPsts 2 rows below, skip 2 sts after the last hdc made] twice, hdc in each of the next 2 sts, popcorn in the next st, hdc in each of the next 2 sts, FPtr in each of the next 2 FPsts 2 rows below, skip 2 sts after the last hdc made, hdc in the next st, hdc in the top of the turning-ch-2, turn.

Row 7: Ch 2, skip the first st, hdc in each of the next 3 sts, [FPdtr in each of the last 2 skipped FPsts 2 rows below, skip 2 sts after the last hdc made, hdc in the next st, FPdtr in each of the next 2 FPsts 2 rows below, skip 2 sts after the last hdc made, hdc in each of the next 5 sts] twice, FPdtr in each of the last 2 skipped FPsts 2 rows below, skip 2 sts after the last hdc made, hdc in the next st, FPdtr in each of the next 2 FPsts 2 rows below, skip 2 sts after the last hdc made, hdc in each of the next 3 sts, hdc in the top of the turning-ch-2, turn.

Row 8: As Row 2.

Repeat Rows 1-8 for the pattern.

FLYING GEESE

Notes

Elongated sc = Insert hook in the ch-sp 3 rows below, yarn over the hook and pull up a loop, stretching it to height required for the current Row, yarn over and draw it through both loops on the hook.

When making an elongated sc, always work over the last two rows.

Always skip the stitch behind an elongated sc.

Chain a multiple of 6 + 2.

Foundation Row (RS): Sc in the second ch from the hook and in each ch across, turn.

Row 1 (WS): Ch 1, sc in each of the first 3 sts, *ch 1, skip the next st, sc in each of the next 5 sts; repeat from the * across ending with ch 1, skip the next st, sc in the last 3 sts, turn.

Row 2: Ch 1, sc in each of the first 3 sts, *sc in the next ch-1 sp, sc in each of the next 5 sts; repeat from the * across, ending with sc in the ch-1 sp, sc in each of the last 3 sts, turn.

Row 3: Ch 1, sc in each sc across, turn.

Row 4: Ch 1, sc in the first st, skip the next 2 sts, elongated sc in the next ch-1 sp 3 rows below, *skip the st after the last sc made, sc in each of the next 3 sts, elongated sc in the same ch-1 sp as the last elongated sc, skip the st after the last sc made, sc in the next st, skip the next 2 sts, elongated sc in the next ch-1 sp 3 rows below; repeat from the * across, ending with skip the st after the last sc made, sc in each of the next 3 sts, elongated sc in the same ch-1 sp as the last elongated st, skip the st after the last sc made, sc in the last st, turn.

Repeat Rows 1-4 for the pattern.

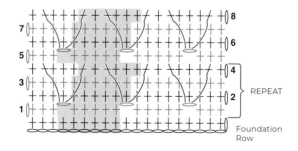

ALTERNATING SPIKES

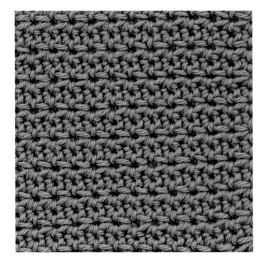

CRINKLE

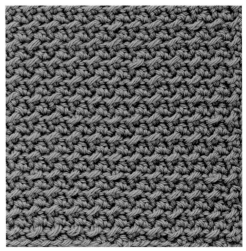

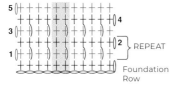

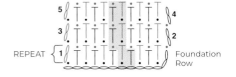

Notes

Elongated sc = Insert hook in the indicated st 2 rows below, yarn over the hook and pull up a loop, stretching it to height required for the current Row, yarn over and draw it through both loops on the hook.

Always skip the stitch behind an elongated sc.

Chain a multiple of 2.

Foundation Row (RS): Sc in the second ch from the hook and in each ch across, turn.

Row 1 (WS): Ch 1, sc in each st across, turn.

Row 2: Ch 1, sc in the first sc, *working over the next sc in the last row, elongated sc in the next sc 2 rows below, sc in the next sc; repeat from the * across, turn.

Repeat Rows 1 and 2 for the pattern.

Chain a multiple of 2 + 1.

Foundation Row (RS): Slip st in the third ch from hook, *hdc in the next ch, slip st in the next ch; repeat from the * across, turn.

Row 1: Ch 2 (counts as hdc here and throughout), skip the first slip st, *slip st in the next hdc, hdc in the next slip st; repeat from the * across, ending with a slip st in the top of the turning-ch-2, turn.

Repeat Row 1 for the pattern.

POSY

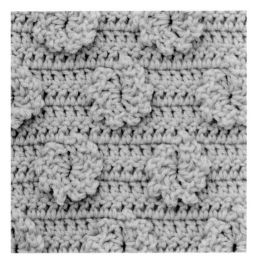

Notes

Posy = Rotating work as needed, work [dc, picot] 5 times down the post of the next dc 1 row below, then work [dc, picot] 4 times up the post of the previous dc 1 row below, dc around the post of the same dc 1 row below.

Do not skip any stitches on Rows 2 and 6; be sure to work in the same dc that you used to create the left side of the posy.

Picot = Ch 3, slip st in the third ch from the hook.

Chain a multiple of 10 + 2.

Foundation Row (RS): Dc in the fourth ch from the hook and in each ch across, turn.

Row 1 (WS): Ch 3 (counts as dc here and throughout), skip the first dc, dc in each dc across, turn.

Row 2: Ch 3, skip the first dc, dc in each of the next 4 dc, *make a Posy, working behind the posy, dc in each of the next 10 dc; repeat from the * across, ending with dc in each of the next 4 dc, dc in the top of the turning-ch3, turn.

Rows 3-5: As Row 1.

Row 6: Ch 3, skip the first dc, dc in each of the next 9 dc, *make a Posy, working behind the posy, dc in each of the next 10 dc; repeat from the * across, ending with dc in each of the next 9 dc, dc in the top of the turning-ch-3, turn.

Rows 7 and 8: As Row 1.

Repeat Rows 1-8 for the pattern.

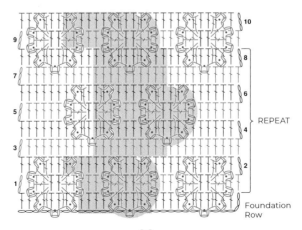

BUCKEYE

Note

Double crochet 5 together (dc5tog) = Yarn over, insert the hook in next st and pull up a loop (3 loops are on your hook); yarn over and draw through 2 loops on the hook; [insert hook in next st and pull up a loop; yarn over and draw it through 2 loops on the hook] 4 times, yarn over the hook and draw loop through all 6 loops on hook. If necessary, use your finger to push the resulting stitch to the right side of the fabric (page 123).

Chain a multiple of 6 + 2.

Foundation Row (RS): Hdc in the third ch from the hook and in each ch across, turn.

Row 1 (WS): Ch 2 (counts as hdc here and throughout), skip the first hdc, hdc in each st across, ending with hdc in the top of the turning-ch-2, turn.

Row 2: Ch 2, skip the first hdc, hdc in each of the next 2 hdc, *5 tr in the next hdc, hdc in each of the next 5 hdc; repeat from the * across, ending with 5 tr in the next hdc, hdc in each of the next 2 hdc, hdc in the top of the turning-ch2, turn.

Row 3: Ch 2, skip the first hdc, hdc in each of the next 2 hdc, *dc5tog over the next 5 tr, hdc in each of the next 5 hdc; repeat from the * across, ending with dc5tog over the next 5 tr, hdc in each of the next 2 hdc, hdc in the top of the turning-ch-2, turn.

Rows 4 and 5: As Row 1.

Row 6: Skip the first hdc, hdc in each of the next 5 hdc, *5 tr in the next hdc, hdc in each of the next 5 hdc; repeat from the * across, ending with, hdc in the top of the turning-ch-2, turn.

Row 7: Skip the first hdc, hdc in each of the next 5 hdc, *5-dc dec over the next 5 tr, hdc in each of the next 5 hdc; repeat from the * across, ending with 5-dc dec over the next 5 tr, hdc in each of the next 5 hdc, hdc in the top of the turning-ch-2, turn.

Row 8: As Row 1.

Repeat Rows 1-8 for the pattern.

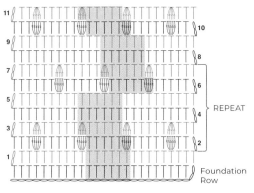

REPEAT

NUBBY

EMBOSSED WEDGES

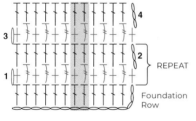

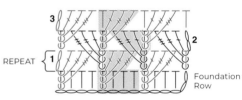

Chain a multiple of 2 + 1.

Foundation Row (RS): Dc in the fourth ch from the hook and in each ch across, turn.

Row 1 (WS): Ch 1, sc in the first dc, *tr in the next dc, sc in the next dc; repeat from the * across, ending with tr in the next dc, sc in the top of the turning-ch-3, turn.

Row 2: Ch 3 (counts as dc here and throughout), skip the first sc, dc in each st across, turn.

Repeat Rows 1 and 2 for the pattern.

Chain a multiple of 4 + 3.

Foundation Row (RS): Hdc in the third ch from the hook and in each ch across, turn.

Row 1: Ch 2, skip the first hdc, *hdc in the next st, [FPdc, FPtr, FPdtr] around the post of the same hdc as where the last hdc was made, skip the next 3 hdc; repeat from the * across, ending with hdc in the top of the turning-ch-2, turn.

Repeat Row 1 for the pattern.

WIDE
HERRINGBONE

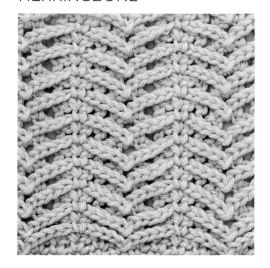

Chain a multiple of 10 + 2.

Foundation Row 1 (RS): Sc in the second ch from the hook, *ch 1, skip the next ch, sc in the next ch; repeat from the * across, turn.

Foundation Row 2: Ch 1, sc in the first sc, *ch 1, skip the next ch-1 sp, sc in the next sc; repeat from the * across, turn.

Foundation Row 3: Ch 1, sc in the first sc, *ch 5, [skip the next ch-1 sp, skip the next sc] twice, working in front of the next ch-1 sp, slip st in the next ch-1 sp 2 rows below, ch 5, skip the next sc, skip the next ch-1 sp] twice, sc in the next sc; repeat from the * across, turn.

Foundation Row 4: Ch 1, sc in the first sc, *[ch 1, skip the next ch-1 sp, working in front of the ch-5 loop of the previous row, dc in the next sc 2 rows below] twice, ch 1, skip the next slip st, [working in front of the ch-5 loop of the previous row, dc in the next sc 2 rows below, skip the next ch-1 sp, ch 1] twice, sc in the next sc; repeat from the * across, turn.

Row 1 (RS): Ch 1, sc in the first sc, *ch 5, [skip the next ch-1 sp, skip the next dc] twice, working in front of the next ch-1 sp, slip st in the next ch-1 sp 2 rows below, ch 5, [skip the next dc, skip the next ch-1 sp] twice, sc in the next sc; repeat from the * across, turn.

Row 2: Ch 1, sc in the first sc, *[ch 1, skip the next ch-1 sp, working in front of the ch-5 loop of the previous row, dc in the next dc 2 rows below] twice, ch 1, skip the next slip st, [working in front of the ch-5 loop of the previous row, dc in the next dc 2 rows below, skip the next ch-1 sp, ch 1] twice, sc in the next sc; repeat from the * across, turn.

Repeat Rows 1 and 2 for the pattern.

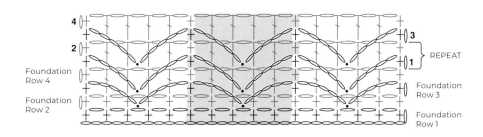

BASKETWEAVE 1

BASKETWEAVE 2

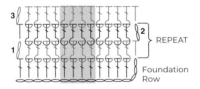

Chain a multiple of 4 + 2.

Foundation Row (RS): Dc in the fourth ch from the hook and in each ch across, turn.

Row 1 (WS): Ch 2 (counts as hdc here and throughout), skip the first st, *BPdc in each of the next 2 sts, FPdc in each of the next 2 sts; repeat from the * across, ending with BPdc in each of the next 2 sts, hdc in the top of the turning-ch, turn.

Row 2: Ch 2, skip the first st, *FPdc in each of the next 2 sts, BPdc in each of the next 2 sts; repeat from the * across, ending with FPdc in each of the next 2 sts, hdc in the top of the turning-ch-2, turn.

Row 3: As Row 2.

Row 4: As Row 1.

Repeat Rows 1-4 for the pattern.

Chain a multiple of 8.

Foundation Row (RS): Dc in the fourth ch from the hook and in each ch across, turn.

Row 1 (WS): Ch 2 (counts as hdc here and throughout), skip the first st, *BPdc in each of the next 4 sts, FPdc in each of the next 4 sts; repeat from the * across, ending with BPdc in each of the next 4 sts, hdc in the top of the turning-ch-2, turn.

Row 2: Ch 2, skip the first st, *FPdc in each of the next 4 sts, BPdc in each of the next 4 sts; repeat from the * across, ending with FPdc in each of the next 4 sts, hdc in the top of the turning-ch-2, turn.

Row 3: As Row 2.

Row 4: As Row 1.

Repeat Rows 1-4 for the pattern.

DIAGONAL STRIPES

Chain a multiple of 6 + 4.

Foundation Row (RS): Dc in the fourth ch from the hook and in each ch across, turn.

Row 1 (WS): Ch 2 (counts as hdc here and throughout), skip the first st, *FPdc in each of the next 3 sts, BPdc in each of the next 3 sts; repeat from the * across, ending with hdc in the top of the turning-ch, turn.

Row 2: Ch 2, skip the first st, *FPdc in each of the next 2 sts, BPdc in each of the next 3 sts, FPdc in the next st; repeat from the * across, ending with hdc in the top of the turning-ch-2, turn.

Row 3: Ch 2, skip the first st, *BPdc in each of the next 2 sts, FPdc in each of the next 3 sts, BPdc in the next st; repeat from the * across, ending with hdc in the top of the turning-ch-2, turn.

Row 4: Ch 2, skip the first st, *BPdc in each of the next 3 sts, FPdc in each of the next 3 sts; repeat from the * across, ending with hdc in the top of the turning-ch-2, turn.

Row 5: Ch 2, skip the first st, *FPdc in the next st, BPdc in each of the next 3 sts, FPdc in each of the next 2 sts; repeat from the * across, ending with hdc in the top of the turning-ch-2, turn.

Row 6: Ch 2, skip the first st, *BPdc in the next st, FPdc in each of the next 3 sts, BPdc in each of the next 2 sts; repeat from the * across, ending with hdc in the top of the turning-ch-2, turn.

Repeat Rows 1-6 for the pattern.

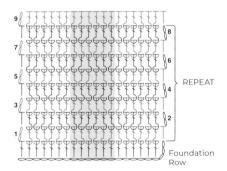

DASHES AND RIBS

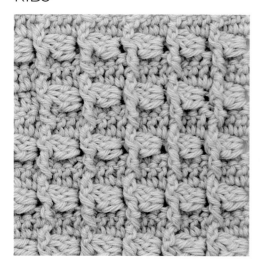

Notes

Foundation Row Cluster (page 125) = [Yarn over and insert hook from front to back to front around the post of the dc 3 sts back, and pull up a loop (3 loops are on the hook), yarn over the hook and draw it through 2 loops] 3 times (4 loops are on the hook), yarn over the hook, insert the hook in the next ch and draw up a loop (6 loops are on the hook), yarn over the hook, and draw it through 2 loops, yarn over and draw it through all 5 loops on the hook.

Main Cluster (page 128) = [Yarn over and insert hook from front to back to front around the post of the dc 3 sts back, and pull up a loop (3 loops are on the hook), yarn over the hook and draw it through 2 loops] 3 times (4 loops are on the hook), [yarn over the hook] twice, insert the hook from front to back to front around the post of the next FPst and draw up a loop (7 loops are on the hook), [yarn over the hook, and draw it through 2 loops] twice, yarn over and draw it through all 5 loops on the hook.

End of Row Cluster (page 124) = [Yarn over and insert hook from front to back to front around the post of the dc 3 sts back, and pull up a loop (3 loops are on the hook), yarn over the hook and draw it through 2 loops] 3 times (4 loops are on the hook), yarn over the hook, insert the hook in the top of the turning-ch-3 and draw up a loop (6 loops are on the hook), yarn over the hook, and draw it through 2 loops, yarn over and draw it through all 4 loops on the hook.

Always skip the st behind each BPtr.

Chain a multiple of 4 + 3.

Foundation Row (RS): Dc in the fourth ch from the hook and in each of the next 2 ch, make a Foundation Row Cluster, *dc in each of the next 3 ch, make a Foundation Row Cluster; repeat from the * across, turn.

Row 1 (WS): Ch 3 (counts as dc here and throughout), *skip the Cluster, dc in each of the next 3 dc, BPtr in the next st; repeat from the * across, ending with skip the Cluster, dc in each of the next 3 dc, dc in the top of the turning-ch-3, turn.

Row 2: Ch 3, skip the first dc, *dc in each of the next 3 dc, make a Main Cluster; repeat from the * across, ending with dc in each of the next 3 dc, make an End of Row Cluster, turn.

Repeat Rows 1 and 2 for the pattern.

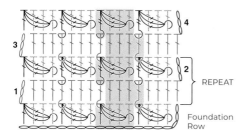

REPEAT

Foundation Row

CHAIN LINKS

Chain a multiple of 5.

Foundation Row 1 (RS): Hdc in the third ch from the hook and in each of the next 2 ch, *ch 10, skip the next ch, hdc in each of the next 4 ch; repeat from the * across, turn.

Foundation Row 2: Ch 2 (counts as hdc here and throughout), skip the first hdc, hdc in each of the next 3 hdc, *keeping the ch-10 loop to the back, tr in the skipped ch of the

Foundation Ch, hdc in each of the next 4 hdc; repeat from the * across, ending with keeping the ch-10 loop to the back, tr in the skipped ch of the Foundation Ch, hdc in each of the next 3 hdc, hdc in the top of the turning-ch-2, turn.

Row 1 (RS): Ch 2, skip the first hdc, hdc in each of the next 3 hdc, *ch 10, skip the next hdc, hdc in each of the next 4 hdc; repeat from the * across, ending with ch 10, skip the next hdc, hdc in each of the next 3 hdc, hdc in the top of the turning-ch-2, turn.

Row 2: Ch 2, skip the first hdc, hdc in each of the next 3 hdc, *keeping the ch-10 loop to the back, tr in the skipped st 2 rows below, hdc in each of the next 4 hdc; repeat from the * across, ending with keeping the ch-10 loop to the back, tr in the skipped st 2 rows below, hdc in each of the next 3 hdc, hdc in the top of the turning-ch-2, turn.

Repeat Rows 1 and 2 for the pattern until the piece measures one Row less than your desired height, ending after Row 1 of the pattern, turn.

Link the chain loops as follows, and then work the final Row below.

To Link the Chain Loops: With the RS facing you, start at the bottom edge, and pull the second chain loop through the first chain loop; pull the third chain loop through the second chain loop; continue in this way until all loops in one vertical section are linked. Repeat for each vertical section.

Last Row: Ch 2, skip the first hdc, hdc in each of the next 3 hdc, *inserting the hook through the top of the next chain loop and in the next tr, hdc in the next tr, hdc in each of the next 4 hdc; repeat from the * across, ending with inserting the hook through the top of the next chain loop and in the next tr, hdc in the next tr, hdc in each of the next 3 hdc, hdc in the top of the turning-ch-2.

Fasten off.

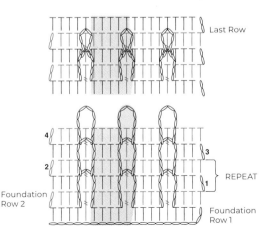

Last Row

4

3

2

REPEAT

1

Foundation Row 2

Foundation Row 1

DIAMOND POPCORN PANEL

Note

Popcorn = 5 dc in the indicated st; drop the loop from the hook; reinsert the hook in the first dc of the 5-dc group, pick up the dropped loop and pull it through the first dc (page 120).

Chain 26.

Foundation Row (WS): Hdc in the third ch from the hook and in each ch across, turn.

Row 1 (RS): Ch 2 (counts as hdc here and throughout), skip the first st, hdc in each of the next 11 sts, popcorn in the next st, hdc in each of the next 11 sts, hdc in the top of the turning-ch-2, turn.

Row 2 and all WS Rows: Ch 2, skip the first st, hdc in each st across, ending with hdc in top of turning-ch-2, turn.

Row 3: Ch 2, skip the first st, hdc in each of the next 9 sts, popcorn in the next st, hdc in each of the next 3 sts, popcorn in the next st, hdc in each of the next 9 sts, hdc in the top of the turning-ch-2, turn.

Row 5: Ch 2, skip the first st, hdc in each of the next 7 sts, popcorn in the next st, hdc in each of the next 3 sts] twice, popcorn in the next st, hdc in each of the next 7 sts, hdc in the top of the turning-ch-2, turn.

Row 7: Ch 2, skip the first st, hdc in each of the next 5 sts, [popcorn in the next st, hdc in each of the next 3 sts] 3 times, popcorn in the next st, hdc in each of the next 5 sts, hdc in the top of the turning-ch-2, turn.

Row 9: Ch 2, skip the first st, hdc in each of the next 3 sts, [popcorn in the next st, hdc in each of the next 3 sts] 5 times, hdc in the top of the turning-ch-2, turn.

Row 11: As Row 7.

Row 13: As Row 5.

Row 15: As Row 3.

Row 16: As Row 2.

Repeat Rows 1-16 for the pattern, ending after Row 2.

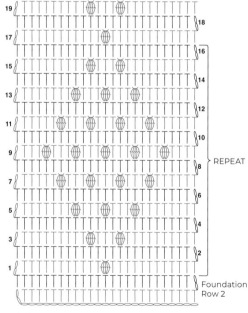

REPEAT

Foundation Row 2

Foundation Row 1

ROPE CABLES

Note

Always skip the hdc behind each FPst.

Chain a multiple of 7 + 3.

Foundation Row 1 (RS): Hdc in the third ch from the hook and in each ch across, turn.

Foundation Row 2: Ch 2 (counts as hdc here and throughout), skip the first st, hdc in each st across, ending with hdc in top of turning-ch-2, turn.

Row 1 (RS): Ch 2, skip the first st, hdc in the next st, *FPtr in each of the next 2 sts 2 rows below, skip 2 sts after the last hdc made, hdc in the next st, FPtr in the next 2 sts 2 rows below, skip 2 sts after the last hdc made, hdc in each of the next 2 sts; repeat from the * across, ending with FPtr in each of the next 2 sts 2 rows below, skip 2 sts after the last hdc made, hdc in the next st, FPtr in the next 2 sts 2 rows below, skip 2 sts after the last hdc made, hdc in the next st, hdc in the top of turn turning-ch-2, turn.

Row 2 and all WS Rows: Ch 2, skip the first st, hdc in each st across, ending with hdc in top of turning-ch-2, turn.

Row 3: Skip the first st, hdc in the next st, *skip the next 3 sts, FPdtr in each of the next 2 sts 2 rows below, skip 2 sts after the last hdc just made, hdc in the next st, working in front of the last 2 FPsts made (page 136), FPdtr in each of the first 2 skipped sts 2 rows below, skip 2 sts after the last hdc made, hdc in each of the next 2 sts; repeat from the * across, ending with skip the next 3 sts, FPdtr in each of the next 2 sts 2 rows below, skip 2 sts after the last hdc made, hdc in the next st, working in front of the last 2 FPsts made, FPdtr in each of the first 2 skipped sts 2 rows below, skip 2 sts after the last hdc made, hdc in the next st, hdc in the top of the turning-ch-2, turn.

Row 4: As Row 2.

Repeat Rows 1-4 for the pattern.

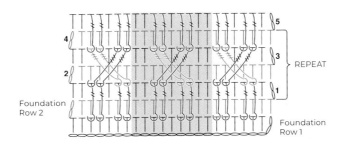

ALIGNED POPCORNS

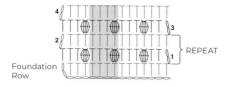

Note

Popcorn = 5 dc in the indicated st; drop the loop from the hook; reinsert the hook in the first dc of the 5-dc group, pick up the dropped loop and pull it through the first dc (page 120).

Chain a multiple of 4.

Foundation Row (WS): Hdc in the third ch from the hook and in each ch across, turn.

Row 1 (RS): Ch 2 (counts as hdc here and throughout), skip the first st, hdc in each of the next 2 sts, *popcorn in the next st, hdc in each of the next 3 sts; repeat from the * across, ending with popcorn in the next st, hdc in each of the next 2 sts, hdc in the top of the turning-ch-2, turn.

Row 2: Ch 2, skip the first st, hdc in each st across, ending with hdc in top of turning-ch-2, turn.

Repeat Rows 1 and 2 for the pattern.

ALTERNATING POPCORNS

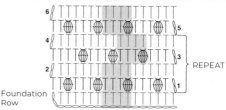

Note

Popcorn = 5 dc in the indicated st; drop the loop from the hook; reinsert the hook in the first dc of the 5-dc group, pick up the dropped loop and pull it through the first dc (page 120).

Chain a multiple of 4 + 2.

Foundation Row (WS): Hdc in the third ch from the hook and in each ch across, turn.

Row 1 (RS): Ch 2 (counts as hdc here and throughout), skip the first st, hdc in the next st, *popcorn in the next st, hdc in each of the next 3 sts; repeat from the * across, ending with popcorn in the next st, hdc in the next st, hdc in the top of the turning-ch-2, turn.

Row 2 and all WS Rows: Ch 2, skip the first st, hdc in each st across, ending with hdc in top of turning-ch-2, turn.

Row 3: Ch 2, skip the first st, hdc in each of the next 3 sts, *popcorn in the next st, hdc in each of the next 3 sts; repeat from the * across, ending with hdc in the top of the turning-ch-2, turn.

Row 4: As Row 2.

Repeat Rows 1-4 for the pattern.

BOBBLES 'N RIBS

Notes

Always skip the hdc behind each FPst.

Each FPtr counts as a FPst.

Popcorn = 5 dc in the indicated st; drop the loop from the hook; reinsert the hook in the first dc of the 5-dc group, pick up the dropped loop and pull it through the first dc (page 120).

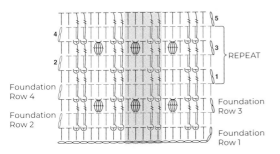

Chain a multiple of 5 + 2.

Foundation Row 1 (RS): Hdc in the third ch from the hook and in each ch across, turn.

Foundation Row 2: Ch 2 (counts as hdc here and throughout), skip the first st, hdc in each st across, ending with hdc in top of turning-ch-2, turn.

Foundation Row 3: Ch 2, skip the first st, hdc in the next st, *FPtr in each of the next 2 sts 2 rows below, skip 2 sts after the last hdc made, hdc in the next st, popcorn in the next st, hdc in the next st; repeat from the * across, ending with FPtr in each of the next 2 sts 2 rows below, skip 2 sts after the last hdc made, hdc in the next st, hdc in the top of the turning-ch-2, turn.

Foundation Row 4: Ch 2, skip the first st, hdc in each st across, ending with hdc in top of turning-ch-2, turn.

Row 1: Ch 2, skip the first st, hdc in the next st, *FPtr in each of the next 2 FPsts 2 rows below, skip 2 sts after the last hdc, hdc in each of the next 3 sts; repeat from the * across, ending with FPtr in each of the next 2 FPsts 2 rows below, skip 2 sts after the last hdc made, hdc in the next st, hdc in the top of the turning-ch-2, turn.

Row 2: Ch 2, skip the first st, hdc into in each st across, ending with hdc into in top of turning-ch-2, turn.

Row 3: Ch 2, skip the first st, hdc in the next st, *FPtr in each of the next 2 sts 2 rows below, skip 2 sts after the last hdc made, hdc in the next st, popcorn in the next st, hdc in the next st; repeat from the * across, ending with FPtr in each of the next 2 sts 2 rows below, skip 2 sts after the last hdc made, hdc in the next st, hdc in the top of the turning-ch-2, turn.

Row 4: As Row 2.

Repeat rows 1–4 for the pattern.

ALLOVER CABLE TWISTS

Notes

This cable panel is worked on a solid hdc ground.

Always skip the hdc behind each FPst.

After Row 1, all FPsts are worked around the posts of FPsts 2 rows below.

Chain a multiple of 22 + 20.

Foundation Row 1 (RS): Hdc in the third ch from the hook and in each ch across, turn.

Foundation Row 2: Ch 2 (counts as hdc here and throughout), skip the first st, hdc in each st across, ending with hdc in the top of the turning-ch-2, turn.

Row 1 (RS): Skip the first st, hdc in each of the next 6 sts, *FPdtr in each of the 2 sts 2 rows below the last 2 sts made, skip 2 sts after the last hdc made, hdc in the next st, skip the next 2 sts, FPdtr in each of the next 2 sts 2 rows below, skip 2 sts after the last hdc made, hdc in each of the next 6 sts, skip the next 3 sts, FPdtr in each of the next 2 sts 2 rows below, skip 2 sts after the last hdc made, hdc in the next st, working in front of the last 2 FPsts made (page 136), FPdtr in each of the last 2 skipped sts 2 rows below, skip 2 sts after the last hdc made, hdc in each of the next 6 sts; repeat from the * across, ending with FPdtr in the 2 sts 2 rows below the last 2 sts made, skip 2 sts after the last hdc made, hdc in the next st, skip the next 2 sts, FPdtr in each of the next 2 sts 2 rows below, skip 2 sts after the last hdc made, hdc in each of the next 6 sts, hdc in the top of the turning-ch-2, turn.

Row 2 and all WS Row: As Foundation Row 2.

Row 3: Ch 2, skip the first st, hdc in each of the next 6 sts, *skip the next 3 sts, FPdtr in the next 2 FPsts 2 rows below, skip 2 sts after the last hdc made, hdc in the next st, working in front of the last FPsts just made, FPdtr in the last 2 skipped FPsts 2 rows below, skip 2 sts after the last hdc made, hdc in each of the next 4 sts, FPdtr in each of the next FPsts 2 rows below, skip 2 sts after the last hdc made, hdc in each of the next 5 sts, FPdtr in each of the last 2 skipped FPsts 2 rows below, skip 2 sts after the last hdc made, hdc in each of the next 4 sts; repeat from the * across, ending with skip the next 3 sts, FPdtr in the next 2 FPsts 2 rows below, skip 2 sts after the last hdc made, hdc in the next st, working in front of the last FPsts just made, FPdtr in the last 2 skipped FPsts 2 rows below, skip 2 sts after the last hdc made, hdc in each of the next 6 sts, hdc in the top of the turning-ch-2, turn.

Row 5: Ch 2, skip the first st, hdc in each of the next 6 sts, *FPtr in each of the next 2 FPsts 2 rows below, skip 2 sts after the last hdc made, hdc in the next st, FPtr in each of the next 2 FPsts 2 rows below, skip 2 sts after the last hdc made, hdc in each of the next 4 sts, FPtr in each of the next 2 FPsts 2 rows below, skip 2 sts after the last hdc made, hdc in each of the next 5 sts, FPtr in each of the next 2 FPsts 2 rows below, skip 2 sts after the last hdc made, hdc in each of the next 4 sts; repeat from the * across, ending with FPtr in each of the next 2 FPsts 2 rows below, skip 2 sts after the last hdc made, hdc in the next st, FPtr in each of the next 2 FPsts 2 rows below, skip 2 sts after the last hdc made, hdc in each of the next 6 sts, hdc in the top of the turning-ch-2, turn.

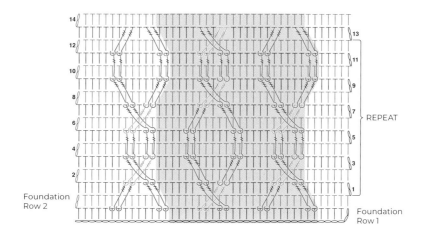

Foundation
Row 2

Foundation
Row 1

REPEAT

Row 7: Ch 2, skip the first st, hdc in each of the next 6 sts, *skip the next 3 sts, FPdtr in each of the next 2 FPsts 2 rows below, skip 2 sts after the last hdc made, hdc in the next st, working in front of the last 2 FPsts made, FPdtr in each of the last 2 skipped FPsts 2 rows below, skip 2 sts after the last hdc made, hdc in each of the next 6 sts, FPdtr in each of the last 2 skipped FPsts 2 rows below, skip 2 sts after the last hdc made, hdc in the next st, skip the next 2 sts, FPdtr in each of the next 2 FPsts 2 rows below, skip 2 sts after the last hdc made, hdc in each of the next 6 sts; repeat from the * across, ending with skip the next 3 sts, FPdtr in each of the next 2 FPsts 2 rows below, skip 2 sts after the last hdc made, hdc in the next st, working in front of the last 2 FPsts made, FPdtr in each of the last 2 skipped FPsts 2 rows below, skip 2 sts after the last hdc made, hdc in each of the next 6 sts, hdc in the top of the turning-ch-2, turn.

Row 9: Ch 2, skip the first st, hdc in each of the next 4 sts, *skip the next 2 sts, FPdtr in each of the next 2 FPsts 2 rows below, skip 2 sts after the last hdc made, hdc in each of the next 5 sts, FPdtr in each of the last 2 skipped FPsts 2 rows below, skip 2 sts after the last hdc made, hdc in each of the next 4 sts, skip the next 3 sts, FPdtr in each of the next 2 FPsts 2 rows below, skip 2 sts after the last hdc made, hdc in the next st, working in front of the last 2 FPsts made, FPdtr in each

of the last 2 skipped FPsts 2 rows below, skip 2 hdc after the last hdc made, hdc in each of the next 4 sts; repeat from the * across, ending with skip the next 2 sts, FPdtr in each of the next 2 FPsts 2 rows below, skip 2 sts after the last hdc made, hdc in each of the next 5 sts, FPdtr in each of the last 2 skipped FPsts 2 rows below, skip 2 sts after the last hdc made, hdc in each of the next 4 sts, hdc in the top of the turning-ch-2, turn.

Row 11: Ch 2, skip the first st, hdc in each of the next 4 sts, *FPtr in each of the next 2 FPsts 2 rows below, skip 2 sts after the last hdc made, hdc in each of the next 5 sts, FPtr in each of the next 2 FPsts 2 rows below, skip 2 sts after the last hdc made, hdc in each of the next 4 sts, FPtr in each of the next 2 FPsts 2 rows below, skip 2 sts after the last hdc made, hdc in the next st, FPtr in each of the next 2 FPsts 2 rows below, skip 2 sts after the last hdc made, hdc in each of the next 4 sts; repeat from the * across, ending with FPtr in each of the next 2 FPsts 2 rows below, skip 2 sts after the last hdc made, hdc in each of the next 5 sts, FPtr in each of the next 2 FPsts 2 rows below, skip 2 sts after the last hdc made, hdc in each of the next 4 sts, hdc in the top of the turning-ch-2, turn.

Row 12: As Row 2.

Repeat Rows 1-12 for the pattern.

DIAMOND ARAN PANEL

Notes

Always skip the hdc behind each FPst.

Popcorn = 5 dc in the indicated st; drop the loop from the hook; reinsert the hook in the first dc of the 5-dc group, pick up the dropped loop and pull it through the first dc (page 120).

Chain 32.

Foundation Row 1 (RS): Hdc in the third ch from the hook and in each ch across, turn.

Foundation Row 2: Ch 2 (counts as hdc here and throughout), skip the first st, hdc in each st across, ending with hdc in the top of the turning-ch-2, turn.

Row 1 (RS): Ch 2, skip the first st, hdc in each of the next 4 sts, FPtr in each of the next 2 sts 2 rows below, skip 2 sts after the last hdc made, hdc in each of the next 6 sts, skip the next 3 sts, FPdtr in each of the next 2 sts 2 rows below, skip 2 sts after the last hdc

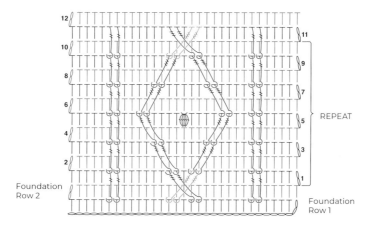

made, hdc in the next st, working in front of the last 2 FPsts just made (page 136), FPdtr in each of the first 2 skipped sts 2 rows below, skip 2 sts after the last hdc made, hdc in each of the next 6 sts, FPtr in each of the next 2 sts 2 rows below, skip 2 sts after the last hdc made, hdc in each of the next 4 sts, hdc in the top of the turning-ch-2, turn.

Row 2 and all WS Rows: Ch 2, skip the first st, hdc in each st across, ending with hdc in the top of the turning-ch-2, turn.

Row 3: Ch 2, skip the first st, hdc in each of the next 4 sts, FPtr in each of the next 2 FPsts 2 rows below, skip 2 sts after the last hdc made, hdc in each of the next 4 sts, skip the next 2 sts, FPdtr in each of the next 2 FPsts 2 rows below, skip 2 sts after the last hdc made, hdc in each of the next 5 sts, FPdtr in each of the 2 skipped FPsts 2 rows below, skip 2 sts after the last hdc made, hdc in each of the next 4 sts, FPtr in each of the next 2 sts 2 rows below, skip 2 sts after the last hdc made, hdc in each of the next 4 sts, hdc in the top of the turning-ch-2, turn.

Row 5: Ch 2, skip the first st, hdc in each of the next 4 sts, FPtr in each of the next 2 FPsts 2 rows below, skip 2 sts after the last hdc made, hdc in each of the next 2 sts, skip the next 2 sts, FPdtr in each of the next 2 FPsts 2 rows below, skip 2 sts after the last hdc made, hdc in each of the next 4 sts, popcorn in the next st, hdc in each of the next 4 sts, FPdtr in each of the 2 skipped FPsts 2 rows below, skip 2 sts after the last

hdc made, hdc in each of the next 2 sts, FPtr in each of the next 2 sts 2 rows below, skip 2 sts after the last hdc made, hdc in each of the next 4 sts, hdc in the top of the turning-ch-2, turn.

Row 7: Ch 2, skip the first st, hdc in each of the next 4 sts, FPtr in each of the next 2 FPsts 2 rows below, skip 2 sts after the last hdc made, hdc in each of the next 4 sts, FPdtr in each of the 2 skipped FPsts 2 rows below, skip 2 sts after the last hdc made, hdc in each of the next 5 sts, FPdtr in each of the next 2 FPsts 2 rows below, skip 2 sts after the last hdc made, hdc in each of the next 4 sts, FPtr in each of the next 2 sts 2 rows below, skip 2 sts after the last hdc made, hdc in each of the next 4 sts, hdc in the top of the turning-ch-2, turn.

Row 9: Ch 2, skip the first st, hdc in each of the next 4 sts, FPtr in each of the next 2 FPsts 2 rows below, skip 2 sts after the last hdc made, hdc in each of the next 6 sts, skip the next 2 sts, FPdtr in each of the 2 skipped FPsts 2 rows below, skip 2 sts after the last hdc made, hdc in the next st, FPdtr in each of the next 2 FPsts 2 rows below, skip 2 sts after the last hdc made, hdc in each of the next 6 sts, FPtr in each of the next 2 sts 2 rows below, skip 2 sts after the last hdc made, hdc in each of the next 4 sts, hdc in the top of the turning-ch-2, turn.

Row 10: As Row 2.

Repeat Rows 1-10 for the pattern.

SAXON BRAID PANEL

Notes

This cable panel is worked on a solid hdc ground.

Always skip the hdc behind each FPst.

Each FPtr and FPdtr counts as a FPst.

Chain 26.

Foundation Row 1 (RS): Hdc in the third ch from the hook and in each ch across, turn.

Foundation Row 2: Ch 2 (counts as hdc here and throughout), skip the first st, hdc in each st across, ending with hdc in top of turning-ch-2, turn.

Row 1 (RS): Ch 2, skip the first st, hdc in each of the next 4 sts, [FPtr in each of the next 2 sts 2 rows below, skip 2 sts after the last hdc made, hdc in each of the next 3 sts, FPtr in each of the next 2 sts 2 rows below, skip 2 sts after the last hdc made, hdc in the next st] twice, hdc in each of the next 3 sts, hdc in the top of the turning-ch-2, turn.

Row 2 and all WS Rows: Ch 2, skip the first st, hdc in each st across, ending with hdc in top of turning-ch-2, turn.

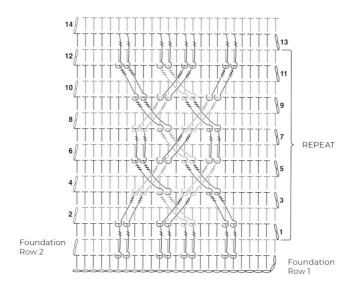

Row 3: Ch 2, skip the first st, hdc in each of the next 6 sts, FPdtr in the last 2 skipped FPsts 2 rows below, skip 2 sts after the last hdc made, hdc in the next st, skip the next 3 sts, FPdtr in the next 2 FPsts 2 rows below, skip 2 sts after the last hdc made, hdc in the next st, working behind the last 2 FPsts made (page 137), FPdtr in each of the last 2 skipped FPsts 2 rows below, skip 2 sts after the last hdc made, hdc in the next st, skip the next 2 sts, FPdtr in each of the next 2 FPsts 2 rows below, skip 2 sts after the last hdc made, hdc in each of the next 6 sts, hdc in the top of the turning-ch-2, turn.

Row 5: Ch 2, skip the first st, hdc in each of the next 6 sts, [skip the next 3 sts, FPdtr in each of the next 2 FPsts 2 rows below, skip 2 sts after the last hdc made, hdc in the next st, working in front of the last 2 FPsts made (page 136), FPdtr in each of the 2 skipped FPsts 2 rows below, skip 2 sts after the last hdc made, hdc in the next st] twice, hdc in each of the next 5 sts, hdc in the top of the turning-ch-2, turn.

Row 7: Ch 2, skip the first st, hdc in each of the next 6 sts, FPtr in each of the next 2 FPsts 2 rows below, skip 2 sts after the last hdc made, hdc in the next st, skip the next

3 sts, FPdtr in the next 2 FPsts 2 rows below, skip 2 sts after the last hdc made, hdc in the next st, working behind the last 2 FPsts made, FPdtr in each of the 2 skipped FPsts 2 rows below, skip 2 sts after the last hdc made, hdc in the next st, FPtr in each of the next 2 FPsts 2 rows below, skip 2 sts after the last hdc made, hdc in each of the next 6 sts, hdc in the top of the turning-ch-2, turn.

Row 9: As Row 5, turn.

Row 11: Ch 2, skip the first st, hdc in each of the next 4 sts, skip the next 2 sts, FPdtr in each of the next 2 FPsts 2 rows below, skip 2 sts after the last hdc made, hdc in each of the next 3 sts, skip the next 3 sts, FPdtr in the next 2 FPsts 2 rows below, skip 2 sts after the last hdc made, hdc in the next st, working behind the last 2 FPsts made, FPdtr in each of the last 2 skipped FPsts 2 rows below, skip 2 sts after the last hdc made, hdc in each of the next 3 sts, FPdtr in each of the last 2 skipped FPsts 2 rows below, skip 2 sts after the last hdc made, hdc in each of the next 4 sts, hdc in the top of the turning-ch-2, turn.

Row 12: As Row 2.

Repeat Rows 1-12 for the pattern.

TREE OF LIFE
PANEL

Notes

This panel is worked on a solid hdc ground.

Always skip the hdc behind the FPst.

Chain 24.

Foundation Row 1 (RS): Hdc in the third ch from the hook and in each ch across, turn.

Foundation Row 2: Ch 2 (counts as hdc here and throughout), skip the first st, hdc in each st across, ending with hdc in the top of the turning-ch-2, turn.

Foundation Row 3: Ch 2, skip the first st, hdc in each of the next 8 sts, skip the next st, FPdtr in the next st 2 rows below, skip the next st after the last hdc made, hdc in the next st, FPtr in the next st 2 rows below, skip the next st after the last hdc made, hdc in the next st, FPdtr in the st one stitch to the left of the last FPst made 2 rows below, skip the next st after the last hdc made, hdc in each of the next 8 sts, hdc in the top of the turning-ch-2, turn.

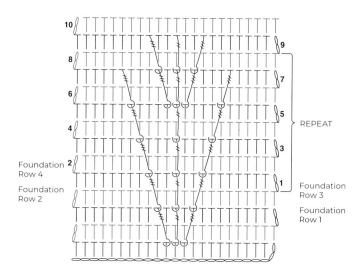

Foundation Row 4: As Foundation Row 2.

Row 1 (RS): Ch 2, skip the first st, hdc in each of the next 7 sts, skip the next st, FPdtr in the next FPst 2 rows below, skip the next st after the last hdc made, hdc in each of the next 2 sts, FPtr in the next FPst 2 rows below, skip the st after the last hdc made, hdc in each of the next 2 sts, FPdtr in the last skipped FPst 2 rows below, skip the st after the last hdc made, hdc in each of the next 7 sts, hdc in the top of the turning-ch-2, turn.

Row 2 and all WS Rows: As Foundation Row 2.

Row 3: Ch 2, skip the first st, hdc in each of the next 6 sts, skip the next st, FPdtr in the next FPst 2 rows below, skip the next st after the last hdc made, hdc in each of the next 3 sts, FPtr in the next FPst 2 rows below, skip the next st after the last hdc made, hdc in each of the next 3 sts, FPdtr in the last skipped FPst 2 rows below, skip the st after the last hdc made, hdc in each of the next 6 sts, hdc in the top of the turning-ch-2, turn.

Row 5: Ch 2, skip the first st, hdc in each of the next 5 sts, skip the next st, FPdtr in the next FPst 2 rows below, skip the next st after the last hdc made, hdc in each of the next 4 sts, FPtr in the next FPst 2 rows below, skip the st after the last hdc made, hdc in each of the next 4 sts, FPdtr in the last skipped FPst 2 rows below, skip the st after the last hdc made, hdc in each of the next 5 sts, hdc in the top of the turning-ch-2, turn.

Row 7: Ch 2, skip the first st, hdc in each of the next 4 sts, skip the next st, FPdtr in the next FPst 2 rows below, skip the next st after the last hdc made, hdc in each of the next 3 sts, skip the next st, FPdtr in the next st 2 rows below, skip the next st after the last hdc made, hdc in the next st, FPtr in the next FPst 2 rows below, skip the next st after the last hdc made, hdc in the next st, FPdtr in the st to the left of the last FPst made 2 rows below, skip the st after the last hdc made, hdc in each of the next 3 sts, FPdtr in the skipped FPst 2 rows below, skip the st after the last hdc made, hdc in each of the next 4 sts, hdc in the top of the turning-ch-2, turn.

Row 8: As Row 2.

Repeat Rows 1-8 for the pattern.

BRAIDED CABLE PANEL

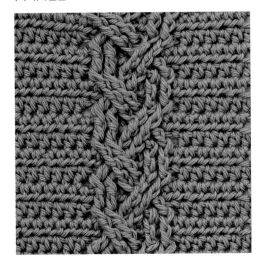

Notes

This cable panel is worked on a solid hdc ground.

Always skip the hdc behind each FPst.

Chain 23.

Foundation Row 1 (RS): Hdc in the third ch from the hook and in the next 5 ch, [dc in each of the next 2 ch, hdc in the next ch] 3 times, hdc in the last 6 ch, turn.

Foundation Row 2: Ch 2 (counts as hdc here and throughout), skip the first st, hdc in each st across, ending with hdc in top of turning-ch-2, turn.

Row 1 (RS): Ch 2, skip the first st, hdc in each of the next 6 sts, skip the next 3 sts, FPdtr in each of the next 2 sts 2 rows below, skip 2 sts after the last hdc made, hdc in the next st, working in front of the last 2 FPsts made (page 136), FPdtr in each of the last 2 skipped sts 2 rows below, skip 2 sts after the last hdc made, hdc in the next st, FPtr in each of the next 2 st 2 rows below, skip 2 sts after the last hdc made, hdc in each of the next 6 sts, hdc in the last ch, turn.

Row 2 and all WS Rows: Ch 2, skip the first st, hdc in each st across, ending with hdc in top of turning-ch-2, turn.

Row 3: Ch 2, skip the first st, hdc in each of the next 6 sts, FPtr in each of the next 2 FPsts 2 rows below, skip 2 sts after the last hdc made, hdc in the next st, skip the next 3 sts, FPdtr in each of the next 2 FPsts 2 rows below, skip 2 sts after the last hdc made, hdc in the next st, working behind the last 2 FPsts made (page 137), FPdtr in each of the 2 skipped FPsts 2 rows below, skip the 2 sts after the last hdc made, hdc in each of the next 6 sts, hdc in the last ch, turn.

Row 4: As Row 2.

Repeat Rows 1-4 for the pattern.

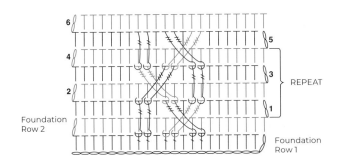

STAGHORN CABLE PANEL

Foundation Row 3: Ch 2, skip the first st, hdc in each of the next 8 sts, FPtr in each of the next 4 sts 2 rows below, skip 4 sts after the last hdc made, hdc in each of the next 8 sts, hdc in the top of the turning-ch-2, turn.

Foundation Row 4: As Foundation Row 2.

Row 1 (RS): Ch 2, skip the first st, hdc in each of the next 6 sts, FPdtr in each of the next 2 FPtr 2 rows below, skip 2 sts after the last hdc made, hdc in each of the next 4 sts, FPdtr in each of the last 2 skipped FPtr 2 rows below, skip 2 sts after the hdc just made, hdc in each of the next 6 sts, hdc in the top of the turning-ch-2, turn.

Row 2 and all WS Rows: Ch 2, skip the first st, hdc in each st across, ending with hdc in top of turning-ch-2, turn.

Row 3: Ch 2, skip the first st, hdc in the next 4 sts, FPdtr in each of the next 2 FPsts 2 rows below, skip 2 sts after the last hdc made, hdc in each of the next 2 sts, FPtr in each of the next 4 sts 2 rows below, skip 4 sts after the last hdc made, hdc in each of the next 2 sts, FPtr in each of the last 2 skipped FPsts 2 rows below, skip 2 sts after the last hdc made, hdc in the next 4 sts, hdc in the top of the turning-ch-2, turn.

Row 4: As Row 2.

Repeat Rows 1-4 for the pattern.

Notes

This cable panel is worked on a solid hdc ground.

Always skip the hdc behind each FPst.

Each FPtr and FPdtr counts as a FPst.

Chain 23.

Foundation Row 1 (RS): Hdc in third ch from the hook and in each ch across, turn.

Foundation Row 2: Ch 2 (counts as hdc here and throughout), skip the first st, hdc in each st across, ending with hdc in top of turning-ch-2, turn.

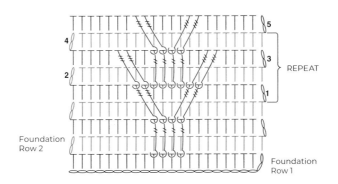

COLORWORK

This section has multicolor fabrics, from checkerboards to textured mosaics to fascinating reversible fabrics. And believe it or not, each one of them, no matter how intricate, is created using just one color per Row!

TONGUE AND GROOVE

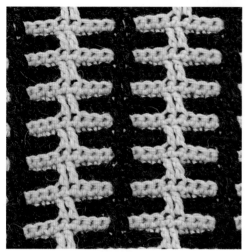

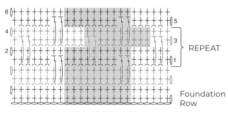

REPEAT

Foundation Row

Notes

This design uses 2 colors: Colors A and B.

Long dc = Double crochet stitch, inserting the hook from the top to the bottom in the front loop only of the indicated stitch 3 rows below.

Always skip the sc behind every long dc.

Change color after every wrong-side row.

With Color A, chain a multiple of 10 + 5.

Foundation Row 1 (RS): Sc in the second ch from the hook and in each ch across, turn.

Foundation Row 2: Sc in each sc across. Change to Color B, turn.

Foundation Row 3: Ch 1, sc in both loops of the first sc, *sc in the back loop only (page 138) of the next sc; repeat from the * across to the last st, ending with sc in both loops of the last st, turn.

Foundation Row 4: As Foundation Row 2. Change to Color A, turn.

Row 1 (RS): Ch 1, sc in both loops of the first sc, sc in the back loop only of each of the next 5 sts, *long dc in each of the next 2 sts 3 rows below, sc in the back loop only of each of the next 8 sc; repeat from the * across, ending with long dc in each of the next 2 sts 3 rows below, sc in the back loop only of each of the next 5 sc, sc in both loops of the last st, turn.

Row 2: Ch 1, sc in each st across. Change to Color B, turn.

Row 3: Ch 1, sc in the first sc, long dc in each of the next 2 sts 3 rows below, *sc in the back loop only of each of the next 8 sc, long dc in each of the next 2 sts 3 rows below; repeat from the * across, ending with sc in both loops of the last sc, turn.

Row 4: As Row 2. Change to Color A, turn.

Repeat Rows 1-4 for the pattern.

HEARTBEATS

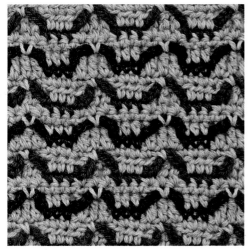

With Color A, chain a multiple of 6 + 4.

Foundation Row 1 (RS): Sc in the second ch from the hook and in each ch across, turn,

Foundation Row 2: Ch 1, sc in each sc across. Change to Color B, ch 1, turn.

Row 1 (RS): Ch 1, sc in each of the first 3 sc, *ch 8, skip the next 3 sc, sc in each of the next 3 sc; repeat from the * across. Change to a second ball of Color A, turn.

Row 2: Ch 2 (counts as hdc here and throughout), skip the first sc, hdc in each of the next 2 sc, *working in front of the ch-8 sp (page 136), tr in each of the next 3 sc, hdc in each of the next 3 sc; repeat from the * across, turn.

Row 3: Ch 1, sc in each of the first 4 sts, inserting the hook under the next ch-8 sp 2 rows below, sc in the next tr, sc in each of the next 5 sts; repeat from the * across ending with sc in the next 3 sts, sc in the top of the turning-ch-2. Change to Color C, turn.

Row 4: As Row 1. Change to Color A from 3 rows below, turn.

Row 5: Ch 2, skip the first sc, hdc in each of the next 2 sc, *working behind the ch-8 sp (page 135), tr in each of the next 3 sc, hdc in each of the next 3 sc; repeat from the * across, turn.

Row 6: Sc in each of the first 4 sts, *insert the hook in the next and also under the next ch-8 sp 2 rows below, complete a sc, sc in the next tr, sc in each of the next 5 sts; repeat from the * across ending with sc in the next 3 sts, sc in the top of the turning-ch-2. Change to Color B, ch 1, turn.

Repeat Rows 1-6 for the pattern, ending after Row 3 or Row 6 of the pattern.

Notes

This design uses 3 colors: Colors A, B, and C.

For ease in finishing and for fewer yarn tails, 2 balls of Color A will be used; when changing to Color A, pick up yarn from the ball that is conveniently waiting for you on the side edge you are working.

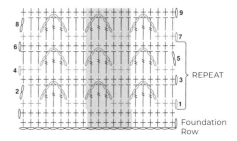

MOROCCAN TILES

Notes

This design uses 2 colors: Colors A and B.

Always work in front of the ch-2 and ch-4 spaces of the previous 2 rows (page 136).

With Color A, chain a multiple of 10 + 3.

Foundation Row 1 (RS): Sc in the second ch from the hook and in each ch across, turn.

Foundation Row 2: Ch 1, sc in each st across. Change to Color B, turn.

Foundation Row 3: With Ch 1, sc in each of the first 2 sc, *ch 2, skip the next sc, sc in each of the next 6 sc, ch 2, skip the next sc, sc in each of the next 2 sc; repeat from the * across, turn.

Foundation Row 4: Ch 1, sc in each of the first 2 sc, *ch 2, skip the next ch-2 sp, sc in each of the next 6 sc, ch 2, skip the next ch-2 sp, sc in each of the next 2 sc; repeat from the * across. Change to Color A, turn.

Row 1 (RS): Ch 1, sc in the first sc, ch 2, skip the next sc, *dc in the next skipped st 3 rows below, sc in each of the next 6 sc, dc in the next skipped st 3 rows below, ch 4, skip the next 2 sc; repeat from the * across, ending with dc in the next skipped st 3 rows below, sc in each of the next 6 sc, dc in the next skipped st 3 rows below, ch 2, skip the next sc, sc in the last sc, turn.

Row 2: Ch 1, sc in the first sc, ch 2, skip the next ch-2 sp, *sc in each of the next 8 sts, ch 4, skip the next ch-4 sp; repeat from the * across, ending with sc in each of the next 8 sts, ch 2, skip the next ch-2 sp, sc in the last sc. Change to Color B, turn.

Row 3: Ch 1, sc in the first sc, *dc in the next skipped st 3 rows below, sc in each of the next 2 sc, ch 2, skip the next sc, sc in each of the next 2 sc, ch 2, skip the next sc, sc in each of the next 2 sc, dc in the next skipped st 3 rows below, repeat from the * across, ending with sc in the last sc, turn.

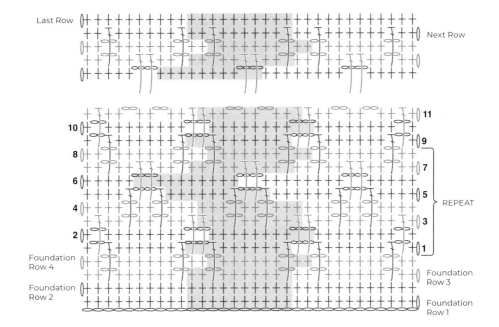

Row 4: Ch 1, sc in the first sc, *sc in each of the next 3 sts, ch 2, skip the next ch-2 sp, sc in each of the next 2 sc, ch 2, skip the next ch-2 sp, sc in each of the next 3 sts; repeat from the * across, ending with sc in the last sc. Change to Color A, turn.

Row 5: Ch 1, sc in each of the first 4 sc, *dc in the next skipped st 3 rows below, ch 4, skip the next 2 sc, dc in the next skipped st 3 rows below, sc in each of the next 6 sc; repeat from the * across, ending with dc in the next skipped st 3 rows below, ch 4, skip the next 2 sc, dc in the next skipped st 3 rows below, sc in each of the last 4 sc, turn.

Row 6: Ch 1, sc in each of the first 5 sts, *ch 4, skip the next ch-4 sp, sc in each of the next 8 sts; repeat from the * across, ending with ch 4, skip the next ch-4 sp, sc in each of the last 5 sts. Change to Color B, turn.

Row 7: Ch 1, sc in each of the first 2 sc, *ch 2, skip the next sc, sc in each of the next 2 sc, dc in each of the next 2 skipped sts 3 rows below, sc in each of the next 2 sc, ch 2, skip the next sc, sc in each of the next 2 sc; repeat from the * across, turn.

Row 8: Ch 1, sc in each of the first 2 sc, *ch 2, skip the next ch-2 sp, sc in each of the next 6 sts, ch 2, skip the next ch-2 sp, sc in each of the next 2 sc; repeat from the * across. Change to Color A, turn.

Repeat Rows 1-8 for the pattern, ending after Row 8 of the pattern. Change to Color A, turn and then work the following two rows.

Next Row (RS): Ch 1, sc in each of the first 2 sc, *dc in the next skipped st 3 rows below, sc in each of the next 6 sc, dc in the next skipped st 3 rows below, sc in each of the next 2 sc; repeat from the * across, turn.

Last Row: Ch 1, sc in each st across. Fasten off.

STREAMERS

Notes

This design uses 2 colors: Colors A and B.

Always work in front of the ch-2 and ch-3 spaces of the previous 2 rows (page 136).

With Color A, chain a multiple of 12 + 11.

Foundation Row 1 (RS): Sc in the second ch from hook and in each ch across, turn.

Foundation Row 2: Ch 1, sc in each sc across. Change to Color B, turn.

Foundation Row 3: Ch 1, sc in the first sc, *ch 3, skip the next 2 sc, sc in each of the next 4 sc; repeat from the * across, ending with ch 3, skip the next 2 sc, sc in the next sc, turn.

Foundation Row 4: Ch 1, sc in the first sc, *ch 3, skip the next ch-3 sp, sc in each of the next 4 sc; repeat from the * across, ending with ch 3, skip the next ch-3 sp, sc in the next sc. Change to Color A, turn.

Row 1 (RS): Ch 1, sc in the first sc, *dc in each of the next 2 skipped sc 3 rows below, sc in each of the next 3 sc, ch 2, skip the next sc, dc in each of the next 2 skipped sc 3 rows below, ch 2, skip the next sc, sc in each of the next 3 sc; repeat from the * across, ending with dc in each of the next 2 skipped sc 3 rows below, sc in the last sc, turn.

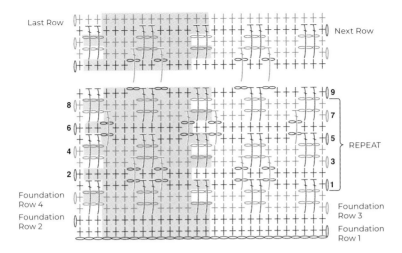

Last Row · Next Row · 9 · 8 · 7 · 6 · 5 · REPEAT · 4 · 3 · 2 · 1 · Foundation Row 4 · Foundation Row 3 · Foundation Row 2 · Foundation Row 1

Row 2: Ch 1, sc in the first sc, sc in each of the next 5 sts, ch 2, skip the next ch-2 sp, sc in each of the next 2 sts, ch 2, skip the next ch-2 sp, sc in each of the next 3 sts; repeat from the * across, ending with sc in each of the last 3 sts. Change to Color B, turn.

Row 3: Ch 1, sc in the first sc, *ch 3, skip the next 2 sts, sc in each of the next 3 sts, dc in the next skipped sc 3 rows below, ch 3, skip the next 2 sts, dc in the next skipped sc 3 rows below, sc in each of the next 3 sts; repeat from * across, ending with ch 3, skip the next 2 sc, sc in the last sc, turn.

Row 4: Ch 1, sc in the first sc, *ch 3, skip the next ch-3 sp, sc in each of the next 4 sts; repeat from * across, ending with ch 3, skip the next ch-3 sp, sc in the last sc, turn. Change to Color A, turn.

Row 5: Ch 1, sc in the first sc, *dc in each of the next 2 skipped sc 3 rows below, ch 2, skip the next sc, sc in each of the next 3 sc, dc in each of the next 2 skipped sts 3 rows below, sc in each of the next 3 sc, ch 2, skip the next st; repeat from * across, ending with dc in each of the next 2 skipped sc 3 rows below, sc in the last sc, turn.

Row 6: Ch 1, sc in the first sc, *sc in each of the next 2 sts, ch 2, skip the next ch-2 sp, sc

in each of the next 8 sts, ch 2, skip the ch-2 sp; repeat from * across, ending with sc in each of the last 3 sts. Change to Color B, turn.

Row 7: Ch 1, sc in the first sc, *ch 3, skip the next 2 sts, dc in the next skipped sc 3 rows below, sc in each of the next 3 sts, ch 3, skip the next 2 sts, sc in each of the next 3 sts, dc in the next skipped sc 3 rows below; repeat from the * across, ending with ch 3, skip the next 2 sts, sc in the last sc, turn.

Row 8: Ch 1, sc in the first sc, *ch 3, skip the next ch-3 sp, sc in each of the next 4 sts; repeat from the * across, ending with ch 3, skip the next ch-3 sp, sc in the last sc. Change to Color A, turn.

Repeat Rows 1-8 for the pattern, ending after Row 4 of the pattern, and then work the following 2 rows.

Next Row (RS): Ch 1, sc in the first sc, *dc in the next 2 skipped sc 3 rows below, sc in each of the next 4 sts; repeat from the * across, ending with dc in each of the next 2 skipped sc 3 rows below, sc in the last sc, turn.

Last Row: Ch 1, sc in each st across.

Fasten off.

GREEK KEY I

Notes

This design uses 2 colors: Colors A and B.

Always work in front of the ch-2 spaces of the previous 2 rows (page 136).

Carry the yarn loosely up the side after each stripe (page 139).

With Color A, chain a multiple of 12 + 4.

Foundation Row 1 (RS): Sc in the second ch from the hook and in each ch across, turn.

Foundation Row 2 (WS): Ch 1, sc in each sc across. Change to Color B, turn.

Row 1 (RS): Ch 1, sc in each of the first 6 sc, *ch 2, skip the next sc, sc in each of the next 11 sc; repeat from the * across, ending with ch 2, skip the next sc, sc in each of the last 8 sc, turn.

Row 2: Ch 1, sc in each of the first 8 sc, *ch 2, skip the next ch-2 sp, sc in each of the next 11 sc; repeat from the * across, ending with ch 2, skip the next ch-2 sp, sc in each of the next 6 sc. Change to Color A, turn.

Row 3: Ch 1, sc in the first sc, *ch 2, skip the next sc, sc in each of the next 3 sc, ch 2, skip the next sc, dc in the next skipped st 3 rows below, ch 2, skip the next sc, sc in each of the next 5 sc; repeat from the * across, ending with ch 2, skip the next sc, sc in the last sc, turn.

Row 4: Ch 1, sc in the first sc, *ch 2, skip the next ch-2 sp, sc in each of the next 5 sc, ch 2, skip the next ch-2 sp, sc in the next st, ch 2, skip the next ch-2 sp, sc in each of the next 3 sc; repeat from the * across, ending with ch-2, skip the next ch-2 sp, sc in the last sc. Change to Color B, turn.

Row 5: Ch 1, sc in the first sc, *dc in the next skipped st 3 rows below, ch 2, skip the next sc, sc in the next sc, ch 2, skip the next sc, [dc in the next skipped st 3 rows below, ch 2, skip the next sc] twice, sc in each of the next 3 sc, ch 2, skip the next sc; repeat from the * across, ending with dc in the next skipped st 3 rows below, sc in the last sc, turn.

Row 6: Ch 1, sc in each of the first 2 sts, *ch 2, skip the next ch-2 sp, sc in each of the next 3 sts, ch 2, skip the next ch-2 sp, sc in the next st] 4 times; repeat from the * across, ending with sc in the last sc. Change to Color A, turn.

Row 7: Ch 1, sc in the first sc, *[ch 2, skip the next st, dc in the next skipped st 3 rows below] 4 times, ch 2, skip the next sc, sc in the next sc, ch 2, skip the next sc, dc in the next skipped st 3 rows below; repeat from the * across, ending with ch 2, skip the next st, sc in the last sc, turn.

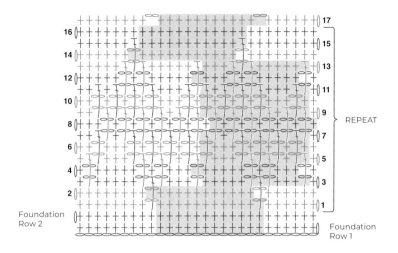

Row 8: Ch 1, sc in the first sc, *ch 2, skip the next ch-2 sp, sc in the next st; repeat from the * across. Change to Color B, turn.

Row 9: Ch 1, sc in the first sc, *dc in the next skipped sc 3 rows below, ch 2, skip the next sc, dc in the next skipped st 3 rows below, sc in the next sc, [dc in the next skipped st 3 rows below, ch 2, skip the next sc] 4 times; repeat from the * across, ending with dc in the next skipped st 3 rows below, sc in the last sc, turn.

Row 10: Ch 1, sc in each of the first 2 sts, *[ch 2, skip the next ch-2 sp, sc in the next st] 4 times, sc in each of the next 2 sts, ch 2, skip the next ch-2 sp, sc in the next st; repeat from the * across, ending with sc in the last sc. Change to Color A, turn.

Row 11: Ch 1, sc in the first sc, *ch 2, skip the next sc, dc in the next skipped st 3 rows below, sc in each of the next 3 sc, [dc in the next skipped st 3 rows below, ch 2, skip the next sc] twice, dc in the next skipped st 3 rows below, sc in the next sc, dc in the next skipped st 3 rows below; repeat from the * across, ending with ch 2, skip the next sc, sc in the last sc, turn.

Row 12: Ch 1, sc in the first sc, *ch 2, skip the next ch-2 sp, sc in each of the next 3 sts, ch 2, skip the next ch-2 sp, sc in the next st, ch 2, skip the next ch-2 sp, sc in each of the next 5 sts; repeat from the * across, ending with ch 2, skip the next sc, sc in the last sc. Change to Color B, turn.

Row 13: Ch 1, sc in the first sc, *dc in the next skipped st 3 rows below, sc in each of the next 5 sts, dc in the next skipped st 3 rows below, ch 2, skip the next sc, dc in the next skipped st 3 rows below, sc in each of the next 3 sc; repeat from the * across, ending with dc in the next skipped st 3 rows below, sc in the last sc, turn.

Row 14: Ch 1, sc in each of the first 6 sts, *ch 2, skip the next ch-2 sp, sc in each of the next 11 sts; repeat from the * across, ending with ch 2, skip the next ch-2 sp, sc in the last 8 sts. Change to Color A, turn.

Row 15: Ch 1, sc in each of the first 8 sts, *dc in the next skipped st 3 rows below, sc in each of the next 11 sc; repeat from the * across, ending with dc in the next skipped st 3 rows below, sc in each of the last 6 sts, turn.

Row 16: Ch 1, sc in each st across. Change to Color B, turn.

Repeat Rows 1-16 for the pattern.

ISTANBUL MOSAIC

Notes

This design uses 2 colors: Colors A and B.

Always work over the ch-2 and ch-4 spaces of the previous 2 rows (page 136).

Carry the yarn loosely up the side after each stripe (page 139).

With Color A, chain a multiple of 8 + 4.

Foundation Row 1 (RS): Sc in the second ch from the hook and in each ch across, turn.

Foundation Row 2 (WS): Ch 1, sc in each sc across. Change to Color B, turn.

Foundation Row 3: Ch 1, sc in the first sc, *sc in each of the next 2 sc, ch 2, skip the next sc, sc in each of the next 3 sc, ch 4, skip the next 2 sc; repeat from the * across, ending with sc in each of the last 2 sc, turn.

Foundation Row 4: Ch 1, sc in each of the first 2 sc, *ch 4, skip the next ch-4 sp, sc in each of the next 3 sts, ch 2, skip the next ch-2 sp, sc in each of the next 2 sc; repeat from the * across, ending sc in the last sc, turn. Change to Color A, turn.

Row 1 (RS): Ch 1, sc in the first sc, *sc in the next sc, ch 2, skip the next sc, dc in the next skipped sc 3 rows below, ch 2, skip the next sc, sc in the next sc, ch 2, skip the next sc, dc in each of the next 2 skipped dc 3 rows below; repeat from the * across, ending with sc in each of the last 2 sc, turn.

Row 2: Ch 1, sc in each of the first 4 sts, *[ch 2, skip the next ch-2 sp, sc in the next st] 3 times, sc in each of the next 2 sts; repeat from the * across, ending with [ch 2, skip the next ch-2 sp, sc in the next st] 3 times, sc in the last sc. Change to Color B, turn.

Row 3: Ch 1, sc in the first sc, ch 2, skip the next sc, *dc in the next skipped sc 3 rows below, sc in the next sc, dc in the next skipped sc 3 rows below, ch 2, skip the next sc, dc in the next skipped sc 3 rows below, sc in the next sc, ch 4, skip next 2 sc; repeat from the * across, ending with ch 2, skip the next sc, sc in the last sc, turn.

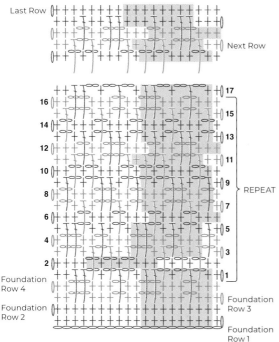

Last Row

Next Row

17
16
15
14
13
12
11
10
9
8
7
6
5
4
3
2
1

REPEAT

Foundation Row 4

Foundation Row 2

Foundation Row 3

Foundation Row 1

Row 4: Ch 1, sc in the first sc, *ch 4, skip the next ch-4 sp, sc in each of the next 2 sts, ch 2, skip the next ch-2 sp, sc in each of the next 3 sts; repeat from the * across, ending with ch 2, skip the next ch-2 sp, sc in the last sc. Change to Color A, turn.

Row 5: Ch 1, sc in the first sc, dc in the next skipped sc 3 rows below, *sc in the next sc, ch 2, skip the next st, sc in the next sc, dc in the next skipped sc 3 rows below, sc in the next sc, ch 2, skip the next sc, dc in each of the next 2 skipped sc 3 rows below; repeat from the * across, ending with sc in the last sc, turn.

Row 6: Ch 1, sc in each of the first 3 sts, *ch 2, skip the next ch-2 sp, sc in each of the next 3 sts; repeat from the * across. Change to Color B, turn.

Row 7: Ch 1, sc in the first sc, *ch 2, skip the next sc, sc in the next sc, dc in the next skipped sc 3 rows below, ch 4, skip the next 2 sc, sc in the next sc, dc in the next skipped sc 3 rows below, sc in the next sc; repeat from the * across, ending with ch 2, skip the next sc, sc in the last sc, turn.

Row 8: Ch 1, sc in the first sc, ch 2, skip the next ch-2 sp, *sc in each of the next 3 sts, ch 4, skip the next ch-4 sp, sc in each of the next 2 sts, ch 2, skip the next ch-2 sp; repeat from the * across, ending with sc in the last sc. Change to Color A, turn.

Row 9: Ch 1, sc in the first sc, *dc in the next skipped sc 3 rows below, ch 2, skip the next sc, sc in the next sc, dc in each of the next 2 sc 3 rows below, ch 2, skip the next sc, sc in the next st, ch 2, skip the next sc; repeat from the * across, ending with dc in the next skipped sc 3 rows below, sc in the last sc, turn.

Row 10: Ch 1, sc in each of the first 2 sts, *ch 2, skip the next ch-2 sp, sc in the next st, ch 2, skip the next ch-2 sp, sc in each of the next 3 sts, ch 2, skip the next ch-2 sp, sc in the next sc; repeat from the * across, ending with sc in the last sc. Change to Color B, turn.

Row 11: Ch 1, sc in each of the first 2 sc, *dc in the next skipped sc 2 rows below, ch 4, skip the next 2 sc, sc in the next sc, dc in the next skipped sc 3 rows below, ch 2, skip the next sc, dc in the next skipped sc 3 rows below, sc in the next sc; repeat from the * across, ending with sc in the last sc, turn.

Row 12: Ch 1, sc in each of the first 3 sts, *ch 2, skip the next ch-2 sp, sc in each of the next 2 sts, ch 4, skip the next ch-4 sp, sc in each of the next 3 sts; repeat from the * across. Change to Color A, turn.

Row 13: Ch 1, sc in the first sc, *ch 2, skip the next sc, sc in the next sc, dc in each of the next 2 skipped sc 3 rows below, ch 2, skip the next sc, sc in the next sc, dc in the next skipped sc 3 rows below, sc in the next sc; repeat from the * across, ending with ch 2, skip the next sc, sc in the last sc, turn.

Row 14: Ch 1, sc in the first sc, ch 2, skip the next ch-2 sp, *sc in each of the next 3 sts, ch 2, skip the next ch-2 sp; repeat from the * across, ending with sc in the last sc. Change to Color B, turn.

Row 15: Ch 1, sc in the first sc, *dc in the next skipped sc 3 rows below, sc in the next sc, ch 2, skip the next sc, sc in the next sc, dc in the next skipped sc 3 rows below, sc in the next sc, ch 4, skip the next 2 sc; repeat from the * across, ending with dc in the next skipped sc 3 rows below, sc in the last sc, turn.

Row 16: As Foundation Row 4: Change to Color A, turn.

Repeat Rows 1-16 for the pattern, ending after Row 12 of the pattern, Change to Color A, turn, then work the following two rows.

Next Row (RS): Ch 1, sc in each of the first 3 sts, *dc in each of the next 2 skipped sc 3 rows below, sc in each of the next 2 sc, dc in the net sc 3 rows below, sc in each of the next 3 sc; repeat from the * across, turn.

Next Row: Ch 1, sc in each st across.

Fasten off.

FAUX CABLES

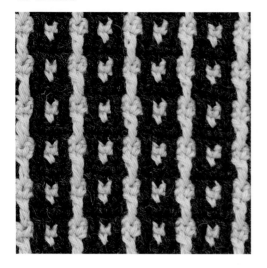

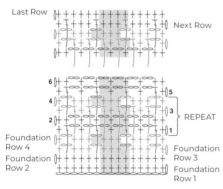

Last Row

Next Row

6
5
4
3
2
1 } REPEAT

Foundation Row 4
Foundation Row 2
Foundation Row 3
Foundation Row 1

Notes

This design uses 2 colors: Colors A and B.

Always work over the ch-2 spaces of the previous 2 rows (page 127).

Carry the yarn loosely up the side after each stripe (page 139).

With Color A, chain a multiple of 4.

Foundation Row 1 (RS): Sc in the second ch from the hook and in each ch across, turn.

Foundation Row 2 (WS): Ch 1, sc in each st across. Change to Color B, turn.

Foundation Row 3: Ch 1, sc in the first sc, *ch 2, skip the next sc, sc in each of the next 3 sc; repeat from the * across, ending with ch 2, skip the next sc, sc in the last sc, turn.

Foundation Row 4: Ch 1, sc in the first sc, *ch 2, skip the next ch-2 sp, sc in each of the next 3 sc; repeat from the * across, ending with ch 2, skip the next ch-2 sp, sc in the last sc. Change to Color A, turn.

Row 1 (RS): Ch 1, sc in the first sc, *dc in the next skipped sc 3 rows below, ch 2, skip the next sc, sc in the next sc, ch 2, skip the next sc; repeat from the * across, ending with dc in the next skipped sc 3 rows below, sc in the last sc, turn.

Row 2: Ch 1, sc in each of the first 2 sts, *ch 2, skip the next ch-2 sp, sc in the next st; repeat from the *across, ending with ch 2, skip the next ch-2 sp, sc in each off the last 2 sts. Change to Color B, turn.

Row 3: Ch 1, sc the first sc, *ch 2, skip the next sc, dc in the next skipped sc 3 rows below, sc in the next sc, dc in the next skipped sc 3 rows below; repeat from the * across, ending with ch 2, skip the next sc, sc in the last sc, turn.

Row 4: Ch 1, sc in the first sc, *ch 2, skip the next ch-2 sp, sc in each of the next 3 sts; repeat from the * across, ending with ch 2, skip the next ch-2 sp, sc in the last sc. Change to Color A, turn.

Repeat Rows 1-4 for the pattern, ending after Row 4 of the pattern, and then work the following 2 rows.

Next Row (RS): Ch 1, sc in the first sc, *dc in the next skipped sc 3 rows below, sc in each of the next 3 sc; repeat from the * across, ending with dc in the next skipped sc 3 rows below, sc in the last sc, turn.

Last Row: Ch 1, sc in each st across.

Fasten off.

SPECIAL REVERSIBLE STRIPES

Note

This design uses 3 colors: Colors A, B, and C.

With Color A, chain a multiple of 5 + 1.

Foundation Row 1 (RS): Dc in the fourth ch from the hook and in each ch across. Change to Color B, turn.

Foundation Row 2: Ch 3 (counts as dc here and throughout), skip the first dc, dc in each of the next 2 dc, *ch 3, skip the next 3 dc, dc in each of the next 2 dc; repeat from the * across, ending with ch 3, skip the next 3 dc, dc in each of the next 2 dc, dc in the top of the turning-ch-3. Change to Color A, turn.

Row 1 (RS): Ch 5 (counts as dc, ch 2 here and throughout), skip the first 3 sts, *working over the ch-2 sp of the previous row (enclosing it inside the fabric) dc in each of the next 3 dc 2 rows below, ch 2, skip the next 2 dc; repeat from the * across, ending with hdc in the top of the turning-ch. Change to Color C, turn.

Row 2: Ch 2 (counts as hdc here and throughout), skip the first hdc, *working over the ch-2 sp, dc in each of the next 2 dc 2 rows below, ch 3, skip the next 3 dc; repeat from the * across, ending with working over the ch-2 sp, dc in each of the next 2 dc 2 rows below, hdc in the second ch of the turning-ch-5. Change to Color A, turn.

Row 3: As Row 1. Change to Color B.

Row 4: As Row 2. Change to Color A.

Repeat Rows 1-4 for the pattern, ending after Row 2 or 4 of the pattern. Change to Color A, then work the last Row as follows.

Last Row (RS): Ch 2, skip the first st, *hdc in each of the next 2 dc, working over the ch-3 sp, dc in each of the next 3 dc 2 rows below; repeat from the * across, ending with hdc in each of the next 2 dc, hdc in the top of the turning-ch-2.

Fasten off.

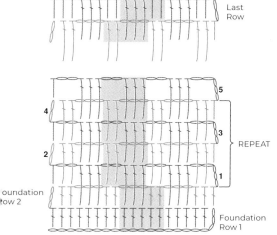

Last Row

5

4

3

2

REPEAT

1

Foundation Row 2

Foundation Row 1

COLORFUL CHECKERBOARD

Notes

This design uses 4 colors: Colors A, B, C, and D.

Always skip the sc behind each dc.

With Color A, chain a multiple of 8 + 1.

Foundation Row 1 (RS): Sc in the second ch from hook and in each ch across, turn.

Foundation Row 2: Ch 1, sc in the front loop only (page 138) of each sc across. Change to Color B, turn.

Row 1 (RS): Ch 1, *sc in the back loop only (page 138) of each of the next 4 sc; dc in the front loop only of each of the next 4 sts 2 rows below; repeat from the * across, turn.

Row 2: Ch 1, sc in the front loop only of each st across. Change to Color C, turn.

Row 3: Ch 1, *dc in the front loop only of each of the next 4 sts 2 rows below, sc in the back loop only of each of the next 4 sts; repeat from the * across, turn.

Row 4: As Row 2. Change to Color D.

Rows 5 and 6: As Rows 1 and 2. Change to Color A.

Rows 7 and 8: As Rows 3 and 4. Change to Color B.

Repeat Rows 1-8 for the pattern.

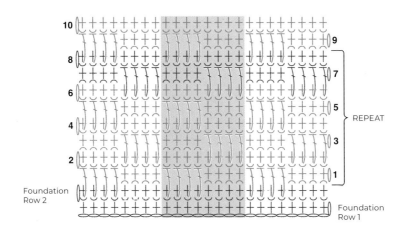

SPIKED STRIPES

Notes

This design uses 3 colors: Colors A, B, and C.

Always skip the hdc behind every FPdc.

Carry the yarn loosely up the side after each stripe (page 139).

With Color A, chain a multiple of 4.

Foundation Row (RS): Sc in the second ch from the hook and in each ch across, turn.

Row 1 (WS): Ch 2 (counts as hdc here and throughout), skip the first st, hdc in each st across, turn. Change to Color B.

Row 2: Ch 1, sc in each of the first 3 hdc, *FPdc in the next st 2 rows below, sc in each of the next 3 hdc; repeat from the * across, ending with FPdc in the next st 2 rows below, sc in each of the next 2 hdc, sc in the top of the turning-ch-2, turn.

Row 3: Ch 2, skip the first sc, hdc in each sc across, turn. Change to Color C.

Row 4: Ch 1, sc in the first hdc, *FPdc in the next st 2 rows below, sc in each of the next 3 hdc; repeat from the * across, ending with FPdc in the next st 2 rows below, sc in the top of the turning-ch-2, turn.

Row 5: As Row 3. Change to Color A.

Rows 6 and 7: As Rows 2 and 3. After Row 7, change to Color B.

Rows 8 and 9: As Rows 4 and 5. After Row 9, change to Color C.

Rows 10 and 11: As Rows 2 and 3. After Row 11, change to Color A.

Row 12: As Row 4.

Repeat Rows 1-12 for the pattern.

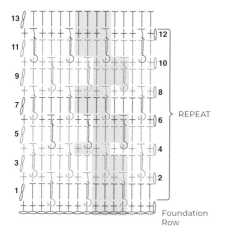

MULTICOLOR RIB

With Color A, chain a multiple of 4.

Foundation Row (RS): Sc in the second ch from the hook and in each ch across, turn.

Row 1 (WS): Ch 2 (counts as hdc here and throughout), skip the first st, hdc in each st across. Change to Color B, turn.

Row 2: Ch 1, sc in each of the first 3 hdc, *FPdc in the next st 2 rows below, sc in each of the next 3 hdc; repeat from the * across, ending with FPdc in the next st 2 rows below, sc in each of the next 2 hdc, sc in the top of the turning-ch-2, turn.

Row 3: As Row 1. Change to Color C.

Row 4: As Row 2.

Row 5: As Row 1. Change to Color A.

Row 6: As Row 2.

Repeat Rows 1-6 for the pattern.

Notes

This design uses 3 colors: Colors A, B, and C.

Always skip the hdc behind every FPdc.

Carry the yarn loosely up the side after each stripe (page 139).

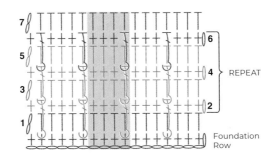

MOSAIC BOXES

Notes

This design uses 2 colors: Colors A and B.

Always work in front of the ch-2 spaces of the previous 2 rows (page 136).

With Color A, chain a multiple of 4.

Foundation Row 1 (RS): Sc in the second ch from the hook and in each ch across, turn.

Foundation Row 2 (WS): Ch 1, sc in each st across. Change to Color B, turn.

Row 1 (RS): Ch 1, sc in the first sc, *ch 2, skip the next sc, sc in each of the next 3 sc; repeat from the * across, ending with ch 2, skip the next sc, sc in the last sc, turn.

Row 2: Ch 1, sc in the first sc, *ch 2, skip the next ch-2 sp, sc in each of the next 3 sts; repeat from the * across, ending with ch 2, skip the next ch-2 sp, sc in the last sc, turn. Change to Color A.

Row 3: Ch 1, sc in the first sc, *dc in the next skipped sc 3 rows below, ch 2, skip the next sc, sc in the next sc, ch 2, skip the next sc; repeat from the * across, ending with dc in the next skipped sc 3 rows below, sc in the last sc. Ch 1, turn.

Row 4: Ch 1, sc in each of the first 2 sc, *ch 2, skip the next ch-2 sp, sc in the next st; repeat from the * across, ending with sc in the last sc. Change to Color B, turn.

Row 5: Ch 1, sc in the first sc, *ch 2, skip the next sc, dc in the next skipped sc 3 rows below, sc in the next sc, dc in the next skipped sc 3 rows below; repeat from the * across, ending with ch-2, skip the next sc, sc in the last sc, turn.

Row 6: As Row 2. Change to Color A.

Row 7: Ch 1, sc in the first sc, *dc in the next skipped sc 3 rows below, sc in each of the next 3 sc; repeat from the * across, ending with dc in the next skipped sc 3 rows below, sc in the last sc, turn.

Row 8: Ch 1, sc in each st across. Change to Color B.

Repeat Rows 1-8 for the pattern.

8

6

4

2

Foundation
Row 2

9

7

5

3

1

REPEAT

Foundation
Row 1

STAIRSTEPS

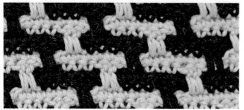

Notes

This design uses 2 colors: Colors A and B.

Always work over the ch-4 spaces of the previous 2 rows (enclosing them inside the fabric).

Carry the yarn loosely up the side after each stripe (page 139).

With Color A, chain a multiple of 7 + 3.

Foundation Row 1 (RS): Sc in the second ch from the hook and in each ch across, turn.

Foundation Row 2: Ch 1, sc in each sc across. Change to Color B.

Foundation Row 3: Ch 1, sc in each of the first 6 sc, *ch 4, skip the next 2 sc, sc in each of the next 5 sc; repeat from the * across, ending with ch 4, skip the next 2 sc, sc in the last sc, turn.

Foundation Row 4: Ch 1, sc in the first sc, *ch 4, skip the next ch-4 sp, sc in each of the next 5 sc; repeat from the * across, ending with sc in the last sc. Change to Color A, turn.

Row 1 (RS): Ch 1, sc in the first sc, *ch 4, skip the next 2 sc, sc in each of the next 3 sc, dc in each of the next 2 skipped sc 3 rows below; repeat from the * across, ending with sc in the last sc, turn.

Row 2: Ch 1, sc in each of the first 6 sts, *ch 4, skip the next ch-4 sp, sc in each of the next 5 sts; repeat from the * across, ending with ch 4, skip the next ch-4 sp, sc in the last sc. Change to Color B, turn.

Row 3: Ch 1, sc in the first sc, *dc in each of the next 2 skipped sc 3 rows below, ch 4, skip the next 2 sc, sc in each of the next 3 sc; repeat from the * across ending with sc in the last sc, turn.

Row 4: Ch 1, sc in each of the first 4 sts, *ch 4, skip the next ch-4 sp, sc in each of the next 5 sts; repeat from the * across, ending with ch 4, skip the next ch-4 sp, sc in each of the last 3 sts. Change to Color A, turn.

Row 5: Ch 1, sc in each of the first 3 sc, *dc in each of the next 2 skipped sc 3 rows below, ch 4, skip the next 2 sc, sc in each of the next 3 sc; repeat from the * across, ending with dc in each of the next 2 skipped sc 3 rows below, ch 4, skip the next 2 sc, sc in each of the last 2 sc, turn.

Row 6: Ch 1, sc in each of the first 2 sc, *ch 4, skip the next ch-4 sp, sc in each of the next 5 sts; repeat from the *across. Change to Color B, turn.

Row 7: Ch 1, sc in the first sc, ch 2, skip the next sc, *sc in each of the next 3 sts, dc in each of the next 2 skipped sc 3 rows below, ch 4, skip the next 2 sc; repeat from the * across, ending with sc in each of the next 3 sts, dc in each of the next 2 skipped sc 3 rows below, ch 2, skip the next sc, sc in the last sc, turn.

Row 8: Ch 1, sc in the first sc, ch 2, skip the next ch-2 sp, *sc in each of the next 5 sts, ch 4, skip the next ch-4 sp; repeat from the * across, ending with sc in each of the next 5 sts, ch 2, skip the next ch-2 sp, sc in the last sc. Change to Color A, turn.

Row 9: Ch 1, sc in the first sc, dc in the next skipped sc 3 rows below, *ch 4, skip the next 2 sc, sc in each of the next 3 sc, dc in each of the next 2 skipped sc 3 rows below; repeat from the * across, ending with ch 4, skip the

Essential Crochet Next-Level Stitches

next 2 sc, sc in each of the next 3 sc, dc in the next skipped sc 3 rows below, sc in the last sc, turn.

Row 10: Ch 1, sc in each of the first 5 sts, *ch 4, skip the next ch-4 sp, sc in each of the next 5 sts; repeat from the * across, ending with ch 4, skip the next ch-4 sp, sc in each of the last 2 sts. Change to Color B, turn.

Row 11: Ch 1, sc in each of the first 2 sc, *dc in each of the next 2 skipped sc 3 rows below, ch 4, skip the next 2 sc, sc in each of the next 3 sc; repeat from the * across, turn.

Row 12: Ch 1, sc in each of the first 3 sc, *ch 4, skip the next ch-4 sp, sc in each of the next 5 sts; repeat from the * across. Change to Color A, turn.

Row 13: Ch 1, sc in each of the first 4 sc, *dc in each of the next 2 skipped sc 3 rows below, ch 4, skip the next 2 sc, sc in each of the next 3 sc; repeat from the * across, ending with dc in each of the next 2 skipped sc 3 rows below, ch 4, skip the next 2 sc, sc in the last sc, turn.

Row 14: Ch 1, sc in the first sc, *ch 4, skip the next ch-4 sp, sc in each of the next 5 sts; repeat from the * across, ending with sc in the last sc. Change to Color B, turn.

Rows 15 and 16: With Color B, as Rows 1 and 2. Change to Color A, turn.

Rows 17 and 18: With Color A, as Rows 3 and 4. Change to Color B, turn.

Rows 19 and 20: With Color B, as Rows 5 and 6. Change to Color A, turn.

Rows 21 and 22: With Color A, as Rows 7 and 8. Change to Color B, turn.

Rows 23 and 24: With Color B, as Rows 9 and 10. Change to Color A, turn.

Rows 25 and 26: With Color A, as Rows 11 and 12: Change to Color B, turn.

Rows 27 and 28: With Color B, as Rows 13 and 14. Change to Color A, turn.

Repeat Rows 1-28 for the pattern, ending after Row 12 or Row 26 of the pattern, and then work the following 2 rows.

Next Row (RS): Ch 1, sc in the first 4 sc, *dc in each of the next 2 skipped sc 3 rows below, sc in each of the next 5 sts; repeat from the * across, ending with dc in each of the next 2 skipped sc 3 rows below, sc in each of the last 3 sc, turn.

Last Row: Ch 1, sc in each sc across.

Fasten off.

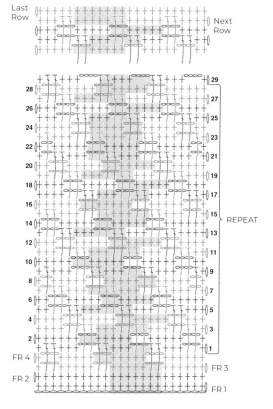

Notes

This design uses 2 colors: Colors A and B.

Always work over the ch-2 spaces of the previous 2 rows (enclosing them inside the fabric).

Carry the yarn loosely up the side after each stripe (page 139).

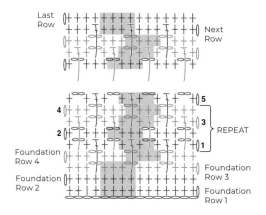

Last Row

Next Row

Foundation Row 4

Foundation Row 2

4

2

5

3

1

REPEAT

Foundation Row 3

Foundation Row 1

With Color A, chain a multiple of 4.

Foundation Row 1 (RS): Sc in the second ch from the hook and in each ch across, turn.

Foundation Row 2: Ch 1, sc in each st across. Change to Color B.

Foundation Row 3: Ch 1, sc in each of the first 3 sc, *ch 2, skip the next sc, sc in each of the next 3 sc; repeat from the * across, turn.

Foundation Row 4: Ch 1, sc in each of the first 3 sc, *ch 2, skip the next ch-2 sp, sc in each of the next 3 sc; repeat from the * across. Change to Color A, turn.

Row 1 (RS): Ch 1, sc in the first sc, *ch 2, skip the next sc, sc in the next sc, dc in the next skipped st 3 rows below, sc in the next sc; repeat from the * across, ending with ch 2, skip the next sc, sc in the last sc, turn.

Row 2: Ch 1, sc in the first sc, *ch 2, skip the next ch-2 sp, sc in each of the next 3 sts; repeat from the * across, ending with ch 2, skip the next sc, sc in the last sc. Change to Color B, turn.

Row 3: Ch 1, sc in the first sc, *dc in the next skipped st 3 rows below, sc in the next sc, ch 2, skip the next sc, sc in the next sc; repeat from the * across, ending with dc in the next skipped st 3 rows below, sc in the last sc, turn.

Row 4: Ch 1, sc in the first 3 sts, *ch 2, skip the next ch-2 sp, sc in each of the next 3 sts; repeat from the * across. Change to Color A, turn.

Repeat Rows 1-4 for the pattern, ending after Row 4 of the pattern. Change to Color A, and then work the following two rows.

Next Row (RS): Ch 1, sc in each of the first 3 sc, *dc in the next skipped st 3 rows below, sc in each of the next 3 sc; repeat from the * across, turn.

Last Row: Ch 1, sc in each st across.

Fasten off.

BROCADE

Foundation Row 1 (RS): Sc in the second ch from the hook and in the next ch, *ch 5, skip the next 2 ch, sc in each of the next 2 ch; repeat from the * across. Change to Color B, turn.

Foundation Row 2: Ch 1, sc in each of the first 2 sc, *working in front of the ch-5 of the previous row (page 136), hdc in each of the next 2 skipped ch in the Foundation Chain, sc in each of the next 2 sc; repeat from the * across, turn.

Row 1 (RS): Ch 1, sc in each st across, turn. Change to Color A.

Row 2: Ch 3 (counts as dc here and throughout), skip the first sc, dc in the next sc, *ch 2, working behind the last row, sc in the next ch-5 sp 3 rows below, ch 2, skip the next 2 sts of the current Row, dc in each of the next 2 sc; repeat from the * across, turn.

Row 3: Ch 1, sc in each of the first 2 dc, *ch 5, skip the next ch-2 sp, skip the next sc, skip the next ch-2 sp, sc in each of the next 2 dc; repeat from the * across, ending with ch 5, skip the next 2 sc, sc in the next dc, sc in the top of the turning-ch-3. Change to Color B, turn.

Row 4: Ch 1, sc in each of the first 2 sc, *working in front of the last 2 rows, tr in each of the next 2 skipped sc 3 rows below, sc in each of the next 2 sc; repeat from the * across, turn.

Repeat Rows 1-4 for the pattern, ending after Row 2 of the pattern.

Notes

This design uses 2 colors: Colors A and B.

Carry the yarn loosely up the side after each stripe (page 139).

With Color A, chain a multiple of 4 + 3.

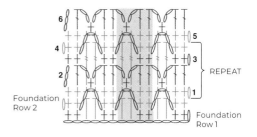

EMBOSSED FISHNET

Foundation Row 2: Ch 1, sc in the first sc, *working in front of the ch-8 of the previous row (page 136), hdc in each of the next 4 skipped ch in the Foundation Chain, sc in the next sc; repeat from the * across, turn.

Row 1 (RS): Ch 3 (counts as dc here and throughout), working behind the ch-8 of the previous row (page 135), skip the first sc, dc in each st across. Change to Color A, turn.

Row 2: Ch 6 (counts as dc, ch 3 here and throughout), working behind the last row, sc in the next ch-8 sp 3 rows below, ch 3, skip the first 5 sc, dc in the next sc, *ch 3, working behind the last row (page 135), sc in the next ch-8 sp, 3 rows below, ch 3, skip the next 4 sts of the previous row, dc in the next sc; repeat from the * across, ending with ch 3, working behind the last row, sc in the next ch-8 sp, 3 rows below, ch 3, skip the next 4 sts of the previous row, dc in the top of the turning-ch-3, turn.

Row 3: Ch 1, sc in the first dc, *ch 8, skip the next ch-3 sp, skip the next sc, skip the next ch-3 sp, sc in the next dc; repeat from the * across, ending with ch 8, skip the next ch-3 sp, skip the next sc, sc in the third ch of the turning-ch-6. Change to Color B, turn.

Row 4: Ch 1, sc in the first sc, *working in front of the last 2 rows, tr in each of the next 4 skipped dc 3 rows below, sc in the next sc; repeat from the * across, turn.

Repeat Rows 1-4 for the pattern, ending after Row 2 of the pattern.

Notes

This design uses 2 colors: Colors A and B.

Carry the yarn loosely up the side after each stripe (page 139).

With Color A, chain a multiple of 5 + 2.

Foundation Row 1 (RS): Sc in the second ch from the hook, *ch 8, skip the next 4 ch, sc in the next ch; repeat from the * across. Change to Color B, turn.

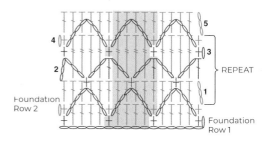

GREEK KEY II

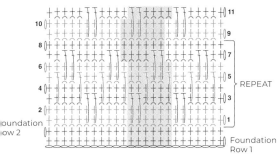

Notes

This design uses 2 colors: Colors A and B.

Long dc = Double crochet stitch, inserting the hook from the top to the bottom in the front loop only of the indicated stitch 3 rows below.

Always skip the sc behind each long dc.

Change color after every wrong-side row.

Carry the yarn loosely up the side after each stripe (page 139).

With Color A, chain a multiple of 6 + 1.

Foundation Row 1 (RS): Sc in the second ch from the hook and in each ch across, turn.

Foundation Row 2: Ch 1, sc in each sc across, turn. Change to Color B.

Row 1 (RS): Ch 1, sc in both loops of the first sc, *sc in the back loop only (page 138) of the next sc; repeat from the * across, ending with sc in both loops of the last sc, turn.

Row 2 and all WS Rows: Ch 1, sc in both loops of each st across, turn. Change color.

Row 3: Ch 1, sc in both loops of the first sc, *sc in the back loop only of each of the next 4 sc, long dc in each of the next 2 sts 3 rows below; repeat from the * across, ending with sc in the back loop only of each of the next 4 sc, sc in both loops of the last sc, turn.

Row 5: Ch 1, sc in both loops of the first sc, *long dc in the next st 3 rows below, sc in the back loop only of each of the next 2 sc; repeat from the * across, ending with long dc in the next st 3 rows below, sc in both loops of the last sc, turn.

Row 7: Ch 1, sc in both loops of the first sc, sc in the back loop only of the next sc, *long dc in each of the next 2 sts 3 rows below, sc in the back loop only of each of the next 4 sc; repeat from the * across, ending with long dc in each of the next 2 sts 3 rows below, sc in the back loop only of the next sc, sc in both loops of the last sc, turn.

Row 8: As Row 2.

Repeat Rows 1-8 for the pattern, ending after Row 8 of the pattern.

INTERLOCKED DIAMONDS

Note

This design uses 2 colors: Colors A and B.

With Color A, chain a multiple of 10 + 5. Place a marker in the eight ch from the hook.

Foundation Row 1 (RS): Dc in the tenth ch from the hook, dc in the next ch, *ch 3, skip the next 3 ch, dc in each of the next 2 ch; repeat from the * across, ending with ch 3, skip the next 3 ch, dc in the last ch. Remove the loop from the hook, and make it large so it doesn't unravel. Do not turn.

Foundation Row 2 (RS): Working in front of the last row (page 136), attach Color B with a slip st to the eight ch (the chain with the marker in it), ch 6 (counts as dc, ch 3 here and throughout), working behind the last row (page 135), dc in the same ch as where the slip st was made, working behind the last row, dc in the center ch of the next ch-3 of the Foundation Ch, ch 3, *working in front of the last row, dc in the same ch of the Foundation Ch as the last dc made, working in front of the last row, dc in the center ch of the next ch-3 of the Foundation Ch, ch 3, working behind the last row, dc in the same ch of the Foundation Ch as the last dc, working behind the last row, dc in the center ch of the next ch-3 of the Foundation Ch, ch 3; repeat from the * across, ending with working in front of the last row, dc in the same ch of the Foundation Ch as the last dc. Remove the loop from the hook, and make it large so it doesn't unravel.

Row 1 (WS): Replace the Color A loop back onto the hook, ch 6, turn. Working behind the last Color B row, dc in each of the next 2 dc worked with Color A, ch 3, *working in front of the last Color B row, dc in each of the next 2 dc worked with Color A, ch 3, working behind the last Color B row, dc in each of the next 2 dc worked with Color A, ch 3; repeat from the * across, ending with working in front of the last Color B row, dc in the last ch-sp of the previous Color A row. Remove the loop from the hook, and make it large so it doesn't unravel. Do not turn.

Row 2 (WS): Keeping the loop in front of the last Color A row, replace the Color B loop onto the hook and ch 6, working behind the last Color A row, dc in the first ch-3 sp of the previous row worked with Color B, working behind the last Color A row, dc in the next ch-3 sp on the previous Color B row, ch 3, *working in front of the last Color A row, dc in the same ch-3 sp as the last dc just made, working in front of the last Color A row, dc in the next ch-3 sp of the previous Color B row, ch 3, working behind the last Color A row, dc in the same sp as the last dc just made, working behind the last Color A row, dc in the next ch-3 sp on the previous Color B row, ch 3; repeat from the * across, ending with

working in front of the last Color A row, dc in the same sp as the last dc on previous Color B row. Remove the loop from the hook, and make it large so it doesn't unravel.

Row 3 (RS): As Row 1.

Row 4 (RS): As Row 2.

Repeat Rows 1-4 for the pattern, ending after Row 2 or 4 of the pattern, then work the next row.

Last Row: Replace Color A onto the hook, turn. Working in front of the last Color B row, sc in the first dc on the previous Color A row, ch 3, working behind the last Color B row, sc in each of the next 2 dc on the previous Color A row, ch 3, *working in front of the last Color B row, sc in each of the next 2 dc on the previous Color A row, ch 3, working behind the last Color B row, sc in each of the next 2 dc on the previous Color A row, ch 3; repeat from the * across, ending with working in front of the last Color B row, sc in the last ch-3 sp.

Fasten off.

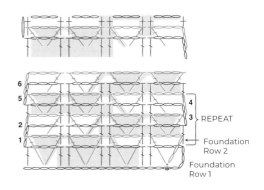

INTERLOCKED STRIPES

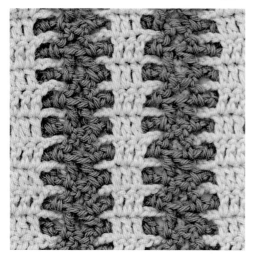

Note

This design uses 2 colors: Colors A and B.

With Color A, chain a multiple of 12 + 4. Place a marker in the eight ch from the hook.

Foundation Row 1 (RS): Dc in the tenth ch from the hook, dc in each of the next 3 ch, *ch 3, skip the next 3 ch, dc in each of the next 3 ch; repeat from the * across, ending with ch 3, skip the next 3 ch, dc in the last ch. Remove the loop from the hook, and make it large so it doesn't unravel. Do not turn.

Foundation Row 2 (RS): Working in front of the last row (page 136), attach Color B with a slip st to the eight ch (the chain with the marker in it), ch 7 (counts as tr, ch 3 here and throughout), working behind the last row, tr in the same ch as where the slip st was made, working behind the last row, tr in the center ch of the next ch-3 of the Foundation Ch, ch 3, *working in front of the last row (page 136), tr in the same ch of the Foundation Ch as the last dc made, working in front of the last row, tr in the center ch of the next ch-3 of the Foundation Ch, ch 3,

working behind the last row, tr in the same ch of the Foundation Ch as the last dc, working behind the last row, tr in the center ch of the next ch-3 of the Foundation Ch, ch 3; repeat from the * across, ending with working in front of the last row, dc in the same ch of the Foundation Ch as the last dc. Remove the loop from the hook, and make it large so it doesn't unravel.

Row 1 (WS): Keeping the hook in front of the last Color B row, replace the Color A loop back onto the hook, ch 6 (counts as dc, ch 3 here and throughout), turn. Working behind the last Color B row, dc in each of the next 3 dc worked with Color A, ch 3, *working in front the last Color B row, dc in each of the next 3 dc worked with Color A, ch 3, working behind the last Color B row, dc in each of the next 3 dc worked with Color A, ch 3; repeat from the * across, ending with working in front of the last Color B row, dc in the last ch-sp of the previous Color A row. Remove the loop from the hook, and make it large so it doesn't unravel. Do not turn.

Row 2 (WS): Keeping the loop in front of the last Color A row, replace the Color B loop onto the hook and ch 7, working in front of the last Color A row, tr in the first ch-3 sp of the previous row worked with Color B, working in front of the last Color A row, tr in the next ch-3 sp on the previous Color B row, ch 3, *working behind the last Color A row, tr in the same ch-3 sp as the last dc just made, working behind the last Color A row, tr in the next ch-3 sp of the previous Color B row, ch 3, working in front of the last Color A row, tr in the same sp as the last dc just made, working in front of the last Color A row, tr in the next ch-3 sp on the previous Color B row, ch 3; repeat from the * across, ending with working behind the last Color A row, tr in the same sp as the last dc on previous Color B row. Remove the loop from the hook, and make it large so it doesn't unravel.

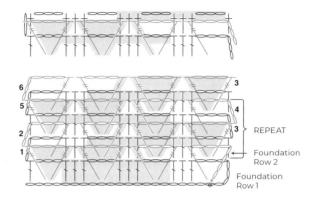

6
5
2
1
3
4
3

REPEAT

Foundation
Row 2

Foundation
Row 1

Row 3 (RS): Replace the Color A loop back onto the hook, ch 6, turn, working in front of the last Color B row, dc in each of the next 3 dc worked with Color A, ch 3, *working in behind the last Color B row, dc in each of the next 3 dc worked with Color A, ch 3, working in front of the last Color B row, dc in each of the next 3 dc worked with Color A, ch 3; repeat from the * across, ending with working behind the last Color B row, dc in the last ch-sp of the previous Color A row. Remove the loop from the hook, and make it large so it doesn't unravel. Do not turn.

Row 4 (RS): Keeping the loop in front of the last Color A row, replace the Color B loop onto the hook and ch 7, working behind the last Color A row, tr in the first ch-3 sp of the previous row worked with Color B, working behind the last Color A row, tr in the next ch-3 sp on the previous Color B row, ch 3, *working in front of the last Color A row, tr in the same ch-3 sp as the last dc just made, working in front of the last Color A row, tr in the next ch-3 sp of the previous Color B row, ch 3, working behind the last Color A row,

tr in the same sp as the last dc just made, working behind the last Color A row, tr in the next ch-3 sp on the previous Color B row, ch 3; repeat from the * across, ending with working in front of the last Color A row, tr in the same sp as the last dc on previous Color B row. Remove the loop from the hook, and make it large so it doesn't unravel.

Repeat Rows 1-4 for the pattern, ending after Row 4 of the pattern, then work the next row.

Next Row (WS): Replace Color A onto the hook, turn. Working in front of the last Color B row, sc in the first dc on the previous Color A row, ch 3, working behind the last Color B row, sc in each of the next 3 dc on the previous Color A row, ch 3, *working in front of the last Color B row, sc in each of the next 3 dc on the previous Color A row, ch 3, working behind the last Color B row, sc in each of the next 3 dc on the previous Color A row, ch 3; repeat from the * across, ending with working in front of the last Color B row, sc in the last ch-3 sp.

Fasten off.

RICK RACK STRIPES

COBBLESTONE

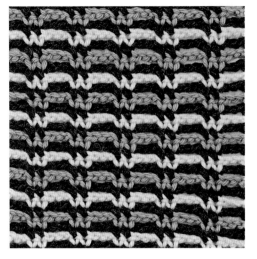

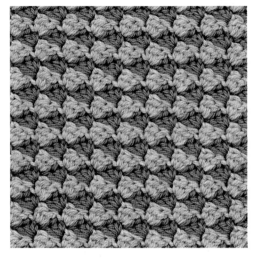

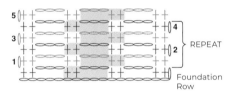

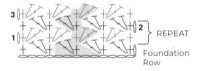

Note

This design uses 3 colors: Colors A, B, and C.

With Color A, chain a multiple of 5 + 3.

Foundation Row (RS): Sc in the second ch from hook and in next ch, *ch 3, skip the next 3 ch, sc in each of the next 2 ch; repeat from the * across. Change to Color B, turn.

Row 1 (WS): Ch 1, sc in each of the first 2 sc, *ch 3, skip next ch-3 sp, sc in each of the next 2 sc; repeat from the * across. Change to Color A, turn.

Row 2: As Row 1. Change to Color C.

Row 3: As Row 1. Change to Color A.

Row 4: As Row 1. Change to Color B.

Repeat Rows 1-4 for the pattern.

Note

This design uses 2 colors: Colors A and B.

With Color A, chain a multiple of 3 + 2.

Foundation Row (RS): [Sc, hdc, dc] in the second ch from the hook, *skip the next 2 ch, [sc, hdc, dc] in the next ch; repeat from the * across, ending with skip the next 2 ch, sc in last ch. Change to Color B, turn.

Row 1 (WS): Ch 1 [sc, hdc, dc] in the first sc, *skip the next 2 sts, [sc, hdc, dc] in the next sc; repeat from the * across, ending with skip the next 2 sts, sc in the last sc. Change to Color A, turn.

Row 2: As Row 1. Change to Color B.

Repeat Rows 1 and 2 for the pattern.

ZIG ZAG
SPIKES

Note

This design uses 3 colors: Colors A, B, and C.

With Color A, chain a multiple of 6 + 2.

Foundation Row (RS): With Color A, sc in the second ch from the hook and in each ch across, turn.

Rows 1-3 (RS): Ch 1, sc in each sc across, turn. After Row 3, change to Color B.

Row 4: Ch 1, sc in the first sc, *working over the previous row (page 132), sc in the next sc 1 row below, working over the previous rows, sc in the next sc 2 rows below, working over the previous rows, sc in the next sc 3 rows below, sc in the next sc 2 rows below, sc in the next sc 1 row below, sc in the next sc; repeat from the * across, turn.

Rows 5-7: As Rows 1-3. After Row 7, change to Color C.

Row 8: As Row 4.

Rows 9-11: As Rows 1-3. After Row 11, change to Color B.

Row 12: As Row 4.

Rows 13-15: As Rows 1-3. After Row 15, change to Color A.

Row 16: As Row 4.

Repeat Rows 1-16 for the pattern.

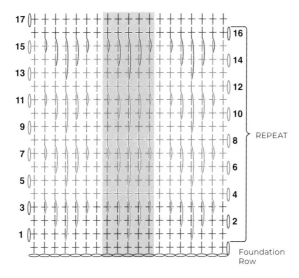

CONFETTI

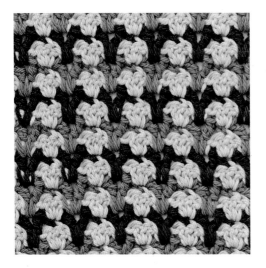

Note

This design uses 3 colors: Colors A, B, and C.

With Color A, chain a multiple of 4 + 2.

Foundation Row 1 (WS): Sc in the second ch from the hook, *skip the next ch, 3 dc in the next ch, skip the next ch, sc in the next ch; repeat from the * across. Change to Color B, turn.

Foundation Row 2: Ch 3 (counts as dc here and throughout), dc in the first sc, *skip the next dc, sc in the next dc, [dc, ch 1, dc] in the next sc; repeat from the * across, ending with skip the next dc, sc in the next dc, 2 dc in the last sc, turn. Change to Color A.

Row 1 (WS): Ch 1, sc in the first dc, *3 dc in the next sc, sc in the next ch-1 sp; repeat from the * across, ending with 3 dc in the next sc, sc in the top of the turning-ch-3. Change to Color C, turn.

Row 2: Ch 3, dc in the first sc, *skip the next dc, sc in the next dc, working over the sc of the previous row (page 132), [tr, ch 1, tr] in the next ch-1 sp 2 rows below; repeat from the * across, ending with skip the next dc, sc in the next dc, 2 dc in the last sc, turn. Change to Color A.

Row 3: As Row 1. Change to Color B.

Row 4: As Row 2. Change to Color A.

Repeat Rows 1-4 for the pattern.

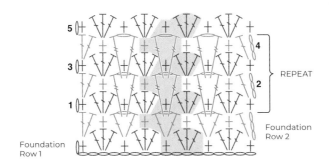

LAYERED BOBBLES

Notes

This design uses 3 colors: Colors A, B, and C.

Long Bobble = Yarn over the hook, insert the hook around the post of next dc from front to back to front and pull up a loop, yarn over the hook, and draw it through 2 loops on the hook, [yarn over the hook, insert the hook from front to back to front around the post of same dc and pull up a loop, yarn over the hook and draw it through 2 loops on hook] 3 times, yarn over the hook and draw it through all 5 loops on hook.

With Color A, chain a multiple of 6.

Foundation Row (RS): Sc in the second ch from hook and in each ch across, turn.

Row 1 (WS): Ch 3 (counts as dc here and throughout), skip the first sc, dc in each st across, turn. Change to Color B.

Row 2: Ch 1, sc in each of the first 5 dc, *long bobble (page 126) in the next dc, skip the dc behind the long bobble just made, sc in each of the next 5 dc; repeat from the * across, ending with long bobble in the next dc, skip the dc behind the long bobble just made, sc in each of the next 4 dc, sc in the top of turning-ch-3, turn.

Row 3: As Row 1. Change to Color C.

Row 4: Ch 1, sc in each of the first 2 dc, *long bobble in the next dc, skip the dc behind the long bobble just made, sc in each of the next 5 dc; repeat from the * across, ending with long bobble in the next st, skip the dc behind the long bobble just made, sc in the next dc, sc in the top of turning-ch-3.

Row 5: As Row 1. Change to Color A.

Row 6: As Row 2.

Row 7: As Row 3. Change to Color B.

Row 8: As Row 4.

Row 9: As Row 1. Change to Color C

Row 10: As Row 2.

Row 11: As Row 3. Change to Color A

Row 12: As Row 4.

Repeat Rows 1-12 for the pattern.

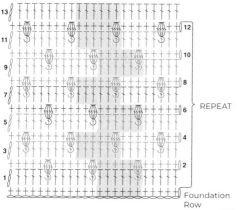

REPEAT

DISCS

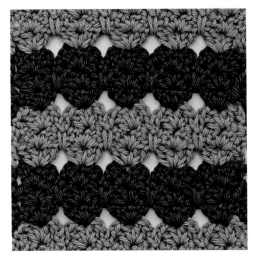

Notes

This design uses 2 colors: Colors A and B.

Shell = [2 dc, ch 1, 2 dc] in same sp.

With Color A, chain a multiple of 5 + 3.

Foundation Row (RS): 2 Dc in the fifth ch from the hook, *ch 1, 2 dc in the next ch, skip the next 3 ch, 2 dc in the next ch; repeat from the * across, ending with ch 1, 2 dc in the next ch, skip the next ch, dc in the last ch, turn.

Row 1 (WS): Ch 3 (counts as dc here and throughout), *shell in the next ch-1 sp; repeat from the * across, ending with dc in the top of turning-ch, turn.

Row 2: Ch 1, sc in the first dc, *ch 2, shell in the next ch-1 sp, ch 2, sc in sp between the next 2 shells 2 rows below; repeat from the * across, ending with ch 2, shell in the next ch-1 sp, ch 2, sc in the top of the turning-ch-3, turn. Change to Color B, ch 3.

Rows 3 and 4: As Row 1.

Row 5: As Row 2. Change to Color A

Row 6: As Row 1.

Repeat Rows 1-6 for the pattern.

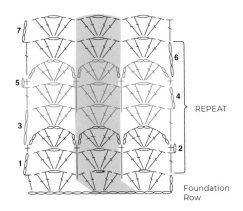

DANCING Vs

Note

This design uses 2 colors: Colors A and B.

With Color A, chain a multiple of 8 + 1.

Foundation Row (WS): Dc in the fourth ch from the hook and in each ch across, turn.

Row 1 (RS): Ch 1, sc in each dc across, ending with sc in the third ch of the turning-ch-3, turn.

Row 2: Ch 1, sc in each sc across. Change to Color B.

Row 3: Ch 1, sc in each of the first 7 sc, *ch 4, sc in the st at base of the next dc 3 rows below, ch 4, skip the next sc from the last row, sc in each of the next 7 sc; repeat from the * across. Change to Color A, turn.

Row 4: Ch 3 (counts as dc here and throughout), skip the first sc, dc in each of the next 6 sc, *dc in the skipped sc 2 rows below, dc in each of the next 7 sc; repeat from the * across, turn.

Rows 5 and 6: As Rows 1 and 2. At the end of Row 6, change to Color B.

Row 7: Ch 1, sc in each of the first 3 sc, *ch 4, sc in the st at base of the next dc 3 rows below, ch 4, skip the next sc from the last row, sc in each of the next 7 sc; repeat from the * across, ending with ch 4, sc in the st at the base of the next dc 3 rows below, ch 4, skip the next sc from the last row, sc in each of the last 3 sc, turn. Change to Color A.

Row 8: Ch 3, skip the first sc, dc in each of the next 2 sc, *dc in the skipped sc 2 rows below, dc in each of the next 7 sc; repeat from the * across, ending with dc in the skipped sc 2 rows below, dc in each of the last 3 sc, turn.

Repeat Rows 1-8 for the pattern.

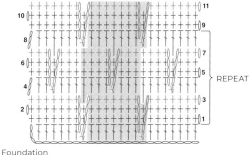

Foundation
Row

REPEAT

UNDULATING PATTERN

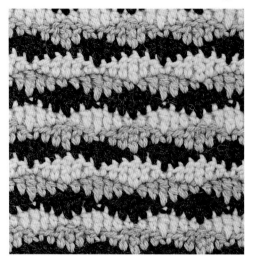

Note

This design uses 3 colors: Colors A, B, and C.

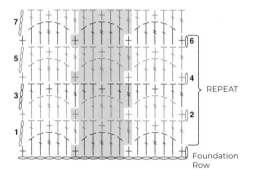

REPEAT

Foundation Row

With Color A, chain a multiple of 6 + 2.

Foundation Row (RS): Sc in the second ch from the hook, *hdc in the next ch, dc in the next ch, tr in the next ch, dc in the next ch, hdc in the next ch, sc in the next ch; repeat from the * across. Change to Color B, turn.

Row 1 (RS): Ch 4 (counts as tr here and throughout), skip the first st, *dc in the next hdc, hdc in the next dc, sc in the next tr, hdc in the next dc, dc in the next hdc, tr in the next sc; repeat from the * across, turn. Change to Color C.

Row 2: Ch 1, sc in the first tr, *hdc in the next dc, dc in the next hdc, tr in the next sc, dc in the next hdc, hdc in the next dc, sc in the next tr; repeat from the * across, ending with hdc in the next dc, dc in the next hdc, tr in the next sc, dc in the next hdc, hdc in the next dc, sc in the top of the turning-ch-4, turn. Change to Color A.

Row 3: With Color A, as Row 1. Change to Color B.

Row 4: With Color B, as Row 2. Change to Color C, ch 4.

Row 5: With Color C, as Row 1. Change to Color A.

Row 6: With Color A, as Row 2. Change to Color B, ch 4.

Repeat Rows 1-6 for the pattern.

ALMOND TILES

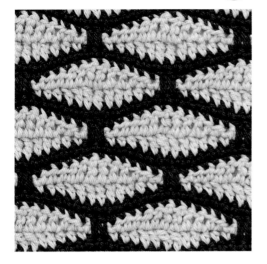

Note

This design uses 2 colors: Colors A and B.

With Color A, chain a multiple of 14 + 13.

Foundation Row (RS): Sc in the second ch from the hook and in each ch across, turn.

Row 1 (WS): Ch 1, sc in each st across, turn. Change to Color B.

Rows 2 and 3: Ch 1, sc in the first st, *hdc in each of the next 2 sts, dc in each of the next 2 sts, tr in each of the next 2 sts, dc in each of the next 2 sts, hdc in each of the next 2 sts, sc in the next st, ch 2, skip the next 2 sts, sc in the next st; repeat from the * across, ending with hdc in each of the next 2 sts, dc in each of the next 2 sts, tr in each of the next 2 sts, dc in each of the next 2 sts, hdc in each of the next 2 sts, sc in the last st, turn. After Row 3, change to Color A.

Row 4: Ch 1, sc in each of the first 12 sts, *working over the ch-2 sp (page 127), dc in each of the next 2 sts 3 rows below, sc in each of the next 12 sts; repeat from the * across, turn.

Row 5: Ch 1, sc in each sc across. Change to Color B, turn.

Row 6: Ch 3 (counts as dc here and throughout), skip the first st, *dc in the next st, hdc in each of the next 2 sts, sc in the next st, ch 2, skip the next 2 sts, sc in the next st, hdc in each of the next 2 sts, dc in each of the next 2 sts, tr in each of the next 2 sts, dc in the next st; repeat from the * across, ending with dc in each of the next 2 sts, hdc in each of the next 2 sts, sc in the next st, ch 2, skip the next 2 sts, sc in the next st, hdc in each of the next 2 sts, dc in the last 2 sts, turn.

Row 7: Ch 3, skip the first st, *dc in the next st, hdc in each of the next 2 sts, sc in the next st, ch 2, skip the next 2 sts, sc in the next st, hdc in each of the next 2 sts, dc in each of the next 2 sts, tr in each of the next 2 sts, dc in the next st; repeat from the * across, ending with dc in the next st, hdc in each of the next 2 sts, sc in the next st, ch 2, skip the next 2 sts, sc in the next st, hdc in each of the next 2 sts, dc in the next st, dc in the top of the turning-ch-3, turn. Change to Color A.

Row 8: Ch 1, sc in each of the first 5 sts, *working over the ch-2 sp, dc in each of the next 2 sts 3 rows below, sc in each of the next 12 sts; repeat from the * across, ending with working over the ch-2 sp, dc in each of the next 2 sts 3 rows below, sc in each of the next 4 sts, sc in the top of the turning-ch-3, turn.

Repeat Rows 1-8 for the pattern.

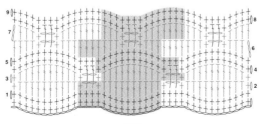

Foundation Row

BARGELLO

Note

This design uses 3 colors: Colors A, B, and C.

With Color A, chain a multiple of 6 + 4.

Foundation Row (RS): Sc in the second ch from hook and in each ch across, turn.

Row 1 (WS): Ch 1, sc in each of the first 3 sc, *ch 1, skip the next st, sc in the next st, ch 1, skip the next st, sc in each of the next 3 sts; repeat from the * across, turn.

Row 2: Ch 1, sc in each of the first 3 sc, *working in front of the last row (page 136), dc in the next st 2 rows below, ch 1, skip the next st, working in front of the last row, dc in the next st 2 rows below, ch 3, skip the next 3 sts; repeat from the * across, ending with dc in the next st 2 rows below, ch 1, skip the next st, dc in the next st one Row below, sc in each of the last 3 sc, turn.

Row 3: Ch 1, sc in each of the first 3 sc, *ch 3, skip the next 3 sts, working behind the last row and keeping the ch-3 in the front, dc in each of the next 3 sts two rows below; repeat from the * across, ending with ch 3, skip the next 3 sts, sc in each of the last 3 sc. Change to Color B, turn.

Row 4: Ch 1, sc in each of the first 3 sc, *working in front of the last row, dc in the next st 2 rows below, tr in the next st 3 rows below, dc in the next st 2 rows below, sc in each of the next 3 dc; repeat from the * across, turn.

Rows 5-7: As Rows 1-3. After Row 3, change to Color C.

Row 8: As Row 4.

Rows 9-11: As Rows 1-3. After Row 11, change to Color A.

Row 12: As Row 4.

Repeat Rows 1-12 for the pattern, ending after Row 4 of the pattern.

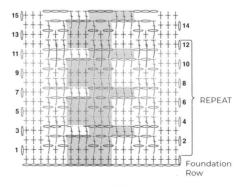

HAPPY HEARTS

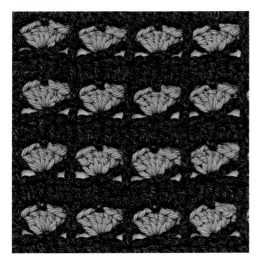

Note

This design uses 2 colors: Colors A and B.

With Color A, chain a multiple of 6 + 2.

Foundation Row (WS): Sc in the second ch from the hook, *ch 2, skip the next 2 ch, dc in the next ch, ch 2, skip the next 2 ch, sc in the next ch; repeat from the * across, turn. Change to Color B.

Row 1 (RS): Ch 3 (counts as dc here and throughout), 2 dc in the first sc, *sc in the next dc, 5 dc in the next sc; repeat from the * across, ending with sc in the next dc, 3 dc in the last sc, turn. Change to Color A.

Row 2: Ch 1, sc in the first dc, *ch 2, skip the next 2 dc, BPdc in the next dc 2 rows below, ch 2, skip the next 2 dc, sc in next dc; repeat from the * across, ending with ch 2, skip the next 2 dc, BPdc in the next dc 2 rows below, ch 2, sc in the top of turning-ch-3, turn.

Row 3: Ch 3, skip the first sc, *2 dc in the next ch-2 sp, dc in the next st; repeat from the * across, turn.

Row 4: Ch 1, sc in the first dc, *ch 2, skip the next 2 dc, dc in the next dc, ch 2, skip the next 2 dc, sc in the next dc; repeat from the * across, ending with ch 2, skip the next 2 dc, dc in the next dc, ch 2, skip the next 2 dc, sc in the top of the turning-ch-3. Change to Color B.

Repeat Rows 1-4 for the pattern.

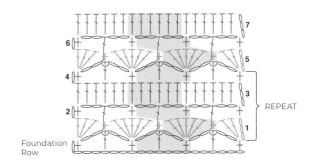

PRETTY PEARLS

Notes

This design uses 2 colors: Colors A and B.

Picot = ch 3, slip st in the top/side of the last dc made (page 130).

With Color A, chain a multiple of 5 + 4.

Foundation Row (RS): [Dc, ch 3, picot, dc] in the fourth ch from the hook, *skip the next 4 ch, [2 dc, picot, ch 1, dc, picot, dc] in the next ch; repeat from the * across, ending with skip next 4 ch, [2 dc, picot, dc] in the last ch, turn. Change to Color B.

Row 1 (WS): Ch 3 (counts as dc here and throughout), dc in the first dc, *ch 2, [dc, ch 2, dc] in the next ch-1 sp; repeat from the *across, ending with ch 2, 2 dc in the third ch of the turning-ch-3, turn. Change to Color A.

Row 2: Ch 2 (counts as hdc here and throughout), skip first 2 dc, *[2 dc, picot, ch 1, dc, picot, dc] in the next ch-2 sp, skip the next ch-2 sp; repeat from the *across, ending with [2 dc, picot, ch 1, dc, picot, dc] in the next ch-2 sp, hdc in the top of the turning-ch-3, turn. Change to Color B.

Row 3: Ch 4 (counts as dc, ch 1 here and throughout), *[dc, ch 2, dc] in the next ch-1 sp, ch 2; repeat from the *across, ending with [dc, ch 2, dc] in the next ch-2 sp, ch 1, dc in the top of the turning-ch-2, turn. Change to Color A.

Row 4: Ch 3 (counts as dc here and throughout), [dc, picot, dc] in the first dc, *skip the next ch-2 sp, [2 dc, picot, ch 1, dc, picot, dc] in the next ch-2 sp; repeat from the * across, ending with [2 dc, picot, dc] in the third ch of the turning-ch-4, turn. Change to Color B.

Repeat Rows 1-4 for the pattern.

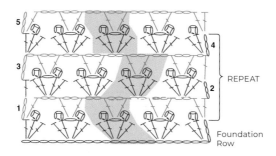

TWO-COLOR SAWTOOTH

Notes

This design uses 2 colors: Colors A and B.

Triangle = Ch 5, sc in the second ch from the hook, hdc in the next ch, dc in the next ch, tr in the next ch.

Triple crochet 2 together (tr2tog) = [Yarn over] twice, insert the hook in next st and pull up a loop (4 loops are on your hook); [yarn over and draw through 2 loops on the hook] twice; [yarn over] twice, insert hook in next st and pull up a loop; [yarn over and draw it through 2 loops on the hook] twice,

yarn over the hook and draw loop through all 3 loops on hook.

With Color A, chain a multiple of 8 + 2.

Foundation Row (WS): Sc in the second ch from hook, *make a triangle, skip the next 4 ch, sc in the next ch; repeat from the * across, turn. Change to Color B.

Row 1 (RS): Ch 4, sc in the top of first triangle, *working in next 4 ch along side of triangle, work sc in the first ch, hdc in the next ch, dc in the next ch, tr in the next ch, sc in the top of the next triangle; repeat from the * across to the last triangle, ending with working in next 4 ch along side of triangle, work sc in the first ch, hdc in the next ch, dc in the next ch, tr2tog over next ch and last sc, turn. Change to Color A.

Row 2: Ch 1, sc in the first st, *make a triangle, skip the next 4 sts, sc in the next tr; repeat from the * across, ending with make a triangle, skip the next 4 sts, sc in the top of the turning-ch-4, turn. Change to Color B.

Repeat Rows 1 and 2 until the piece measures approximately one row less than the desired length, ending after Row 1 of the pattern. Do not change color.

Next Row (WS): Ch 1, sc in the first st, *ch 4, skip the next 4 sts, sc in the next tr; repeat from the * across, ending with ch 4, skip the next 4 sts, sc in the top of the turning-ch-4.

Fasten off.

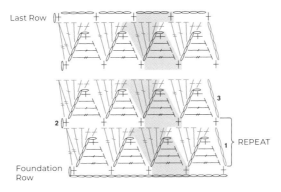

Last Row

Foundation Row

REPEAT

PEAKS AND VALLEYS

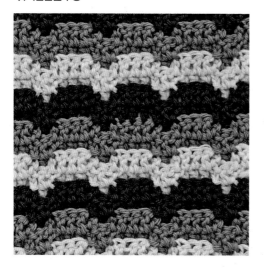

Note

This design uses 3 colors: Colors A, B, and C.

With Color A, chain a multiple of 10 + 7.

Foundation Row (RS): Dc in the fourth ch from the hook and in each of the next 2 ch, ch 3, slip st in the next ch, *skip the next 2 ch, dc in the next ch, skip the next 2 ch, slip st in the next ch, ch 3, dc in each of the next 3 ch, ch 3, slip st in the next ch; repeat from the * across, ending with skip the next 2 ch, dc in the next ch, skip the next 2 ch, slip st in the next ch, ch 3, dc in each of the last 4 ch, turn.

Foundation Row 2: Ch 3 (counts as dc here and throughout), skip the first dc, *dc in each of the next 3 dc, ch 2, slip st in the top of the next ch-3, dc in the next dc, slip st in the top of the next ch-3, ch 2; repeat from the * across, ending with dc in each of the next 3 dc, dc in the top of the turning-ch-3, turn. Change to Color B.

Row 1 (RS): Ch 3, skip the first dc, *dc in the back loop only (page 138) of each of the next 3 dc, ch 2, slip st in the top of the next ch-3, dc in the back loop only of the next dc, slip st in the top of the next ch-3, ch 2; repeat from the * across, ending with dc in the back loop only of each of the next 3 dc, dc in the top of the turning-ch-3, turn.

Row 2: Ch 3, skip the first dc, *dc in each of the next 3 dc, ch 2, slip st in the top of the next ch-3, dc in the next dc, slip st in the top of the next ch-3, ch 2; repeat from the * across, ending with dc in each of the next 3 dc, dc in the top of the turning-ch-3, turn. Change to Color C.

Rows 3 and 4: As Rows 1 and 2. Change to Color A.

Rows 5 and 6: As Rows 1 and 2. Change to Color B.

Repeat Rows 1-6 for the pattern.

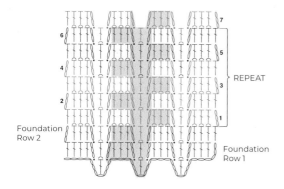

TONAL SHELLS

Note

This design uses 3 colors: Colors A, B, and C.

With Color A, chain a multiple of 10 + 2.

Foundation Row (RS): Sc in the second ch from hook and in each ch across, turn. Change to Color B.

Row 1 (WS): Ch 1, sc in the first sc, *skip the next 4 sc, 7 tr in the next sc, skip the next 4 sc, sc in the next sc; repeat from the * across, turn. Change to Color A.

Row 2: Ch 1, sc in each st across, turn. Change to Color C.

Row 3: Ch 4 (counts as tr here and throughout), 3 tr in the first sc, *skip the next 3 sc, sc in the next sc, skip the next 3 sc, 7 tr in the next sc; repeat from the * across, ending with skip the next 3 sc, sc in the next sc, skip the next 3 sc, 4 tr in the last sc, turn. Change to Color A.

Row 4: As Row 2. Change to Color B.

Repeat Rows 1-4 for the pattern.

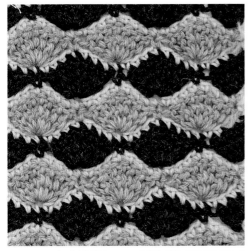

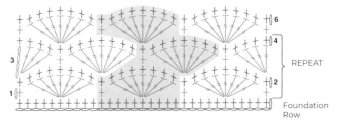

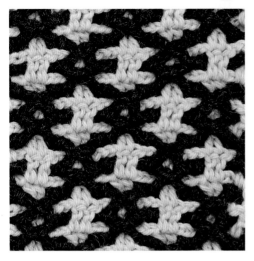

Notes

This design uses 2 colors: Colors A and B.

This pattern is made of two interlocking layers of fabric, each using a different color.

Each Row is worked in the stitches or spaces on the last row of the same color. You will never be working Color A in a stitch or space worked with Color B.

With Color A, chain a multiple of 10 + 5. Place a marker in the eight ch from the hook.

Foundation Row 1 (RS): Dc in the tenth ch from the hook, dc in the next ch, *ch 3, skip the next 3 ch, dc in each of the next 2 ch; repeat from the * across, ending with ch 3, skip the next 3 ch, dc in the last ch. Remove the loop from the hook, and make it large so it doesn't unravel. Do not turn.

Foundation Row 2 (RS): Working in front of the last row, attach Color B with a slip st to the eight ch (the chain with the marker in it), ch 6, working behind the last row (page 135), dc in the same ch as where the slip st was made, working behind the last row, dc in the center ch of the next ch-3 of the Foundation Ch, ch 3, *working in front of the last row (page 136), dc in the same ch of the

Foundation Ch as the last dc made, working in front of the last row, dc in the center ch of the next ch-3 of the Foundation Ch, ch 3, working behind the last row, dc in the same ch of the Foundation Ch as the last dc, working behind the last row, dc in the center ch of the next ch-3 of the Foundation Ch, ch 3; repeat from the * across, ending with working in front of the last row, dc in the same ch of the Foundation Ch as the last dc. Remove the loop from the hook, and make it large so it doesn't unravel.

Row 1 (WS): Replace the Color A loop back onto the hook, ch 6, turn. Working behind the last Color B row, dc in each of the next 2 dc worked with Color A, ch 3, *working in front the last Color B row, dc in each of the next 2 dc worked with Color A, ch 3, working behind the last Color B row, dc in each of the next 2 dc worked with Color A, ch 3; repeat from the * across, ending with working in front of the last Color B row, dc in the last ch-sp of the previous Color A row. Remove the loop from the hook, and make it large so it doesn't unravel. Do not turn.

Row 2 (WS): Keeping the loop in front of the last Color A row, replace the Color B loop onto the hook and ch 6 (counts as dc, ch 3 here and throughout), working in front of the last Color A row, dc in the first ch-3 sp of the previous row worked with Color B, working in front of the last Color A row, dc in the next ch-3 sp on the previous Color B row, ch 3, *working behind the last Color A row, dc in the same ch-3 sp as the last dc just made, working behind the last Color A row, dc in the next ch-3 sp of the previous Color B row, ch 3, working in front of the last Color A row, dc in the same sp as the last dc just made, working in front of the last Color A row, dc in the next ch-3 sp on the previous Color B row, ch 3; repeat from the * across, ending with working behind the last Color A row, dc in the same sp as the last dc on previous Color B row. Remove the loop from the hook, and make it large so it doesn't unravel.

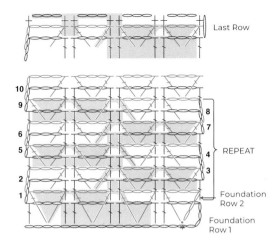

Row 3 (RS): Replace the Color A loop back onto the hook, ch 6, turn, working in front of the last Color B row, dc in each of the next 2 dc worked with Color A, ch 3, *working behind the last Color B row, dc in each of the next 2 dc worked with Color A, ch 3, working in front of the last Color B row, dc in each of the next 2 dc worked with Color A, ch 3; repeat from the * across, ending with working behind the last Color B row, dc in the last ch-sp of the previous Color A row. Remove the loop from the hook, and make it large so it doesn't unravel. Do not turn.

Row 4 (RS): As Row 2.

Row 5 (WS): As Row 3.

Row 6 (WS): Keeping the loop in front of the last Color A row, replace the Color B loop onto the hook and ch 6, working behind the last Color A row, dc in the first ch-3 sp of the previous row worked with Color B, working behind the last Color A row, dc in the next ch-3 sp on the previous Color B row, ch 3, *working in front of the last Color A row, dc in the same ch-3 sp as the last dc just made, working in front of the last Color A row, dc in the next ch-3 sp of the previous Color B row, ch 3, working behind the last Color A row,

dc in the same sp as the last dc just made, working behind the last Color A row, dc in the next ch-3 sp on the previous Color B row, ch 3; repeat from the * across, ending with working in front of the last Color A row, dc in the same ch-sp as the last dc on previous Color B row. Remove the loop from the hook, and make it large so it doesn't unravel.

Row 7 (RS): As Row 1.

Row 8 (RS): As Row 6.

Repeat Rows 1-8 for the pattern, ending after Row 6 of the pattern, then work the next row.

Last Row (RS): Replace Color A onto the hook, turn, working behind the last Color B row, sc in the first dc on the previous Color A row, ch 3, working in front of the last Color B row, sc in each of the next 2 dc on the previous Color A row, ch 3, *working behind the last Color B row, sc in each of the next 2 dc on the previous Color A row, ch 3, working in front of the last Color B row, sc in each of the next 2 dc on the previous Color A row, ch 3; repeat from the * across, ending with working behind the last Color B row, sc in the last ch-3 sp.

Fasten off.

The Stitch Collection: Colorwork

SNAZZY SHELLS

Notes

This design uses 3 colors: Colors A, B, and C. Always work over the ch-spaces of the previous 2 rows (enclosing them inside the fabric).

With Color A, chain a multiple of 6 + 4.

Foundation Row 1 (RS): 2 dc in the fourth ch from the hook, *ch 3, skip the next 5 ch, 5 dc in the next ch; repeat from the * across, ending with ch 3, skip the next 5 ch, 3 dc in the last ch, turn.

Foundation Row 2: Ch 1, sc in each of the first 3 dc, *ch 3, sc in each of the next 5 dc; repeat from the * across, ending with ch 3, sc in each of the next 2 dc, sc in the top of the turning-ch-3, turn. Change to Color B.

Foundation Row 3: Ch 1, sc in the first sc, *ch 2, skip one ch of the Foundation Chain, dc in each of the next 3 ch of the Foundation Chain, ch 2, skip the next 2 sc, sc in the next sc; repeat from the * across, turn. Change to Color C.

Row 1 (WS): Ch 1, sc in the first sc, ch 1, *skip the next dc, 5 dc in the next dc, ch 3, skip the next ch-2 sp, skip the next sc, skip the next ch-2 sp; repeat from the * across, ending with skip the next dc, 5 dc in the next sc, ch 1, skip the next dc, skip the next ch-sp, sc in the last sc, turn.

Row 2: Ch 1, sc in the first sc, ch 1, skip the next ch-1 sp, *sc in each of the next 5 dc, ch 3; repeat from the *across, ending with sc in each of the next 5 dc, ch 1, skip the next ch-1 sp, sc in the last sc, turn. Change to Color B.

Row 3: Ch 1, sc in the first sc, dc in the next ch-1 sp 3 rows below, *ch 2, skip the next 2 sc, sc in the next sc, ch 2, dc in the next ch-2 sp 3 rows below, dc in the next sc 3 rows below, dc in the next ch-2 sp 3 rows below; repeat from the *across, ending with ch 2, skip the next 2 sc, sc in the next sc, ch 2, dc in the next ch-sp 3 rows below, sc in the last sc, turn. Change to Color A.

Row 4: Ch 3 (counts as dc here and throughout), 2 dc in the first sc, *ch 3, skip the next ch-2 sp, skip the next sc, skip the next ch-2 sp, skip the next dc, 5 dc in the next dc; repeat from the * across, ending with ch 3, skip the next ch-2 sp, skip the next sc, skip the next ch-2 sp, skip the next dc, 3 dc in the last sc, turn.

Row 5: Ch 1, sc in each of the first 3 dc, *ch 3, skip the next ch-3 sp, sc in each of the next 5 dc; repeat from the *across, ending with ch 3, skip the next ch-3 sp, sc in each of the next 2 dc, sc in the third ch of the turning-ch-3, turn. Change to Color B.

Row 6: Ch 1, sc in the first sc, *ch 2, skip the next 2 sc, skip the next ch-3 sp, dc in the next ch-2 sp 3 rows below, dc in the next sc 3 rows below, dc in the next ch-2 sp 3 rows below, ch 2, skip the next 2 sc, sc in the next sc; repeat from the * across, turn. Change to Color C.

Repeat Rows 1-6 for the pattern, ending after Row 3 or 6 of the pattern.

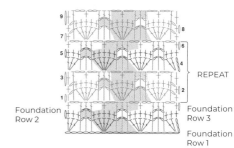

FANCY EDGINGS

Synonymous with the idea of "crochet" to so many people, here's a collection of edgings that can be sewn on to an article to provide the perfect finishing touch. Or, stitch them directly onto the edge of a project as a border. Just ignore the instructions for the foundation chain and begin with the first row of the pattern!

EDGING 1

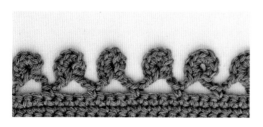

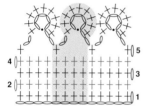

Chain a multiple of 4 + 2.

Row 1 (RS): Sc in the second ch from the hook and in each ch across, turn.

Rows 2-4: Ch 1, sc in each sc across, turn.

Row 5: Ch 1, sc in the first sc, *ch 7, slip st in the fifth ch from the hook, 9 sc in the ch-5 loop just made by the last slip st, ch 2, skip the next 3 sc, sc in the next sc; repeat from the * across.

Fasten off.

EDGING 2

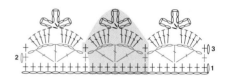

Chain a multiple of 8 + 2.

Row 1 (RS): Sc in the second ch from the hook and in each ch across, turn.

Row 2: Ch 1, sc in the first sc, *ch 1, skip the next 3 sc, [(dc, ch 3) twice, dc] in the next ch, ch 1, skip the next 3 sc, sc in the next sc; repeat from the * across, turn.

Row 3: Ch 1, sc in the first sc, *5 dc in the next ch-3 sp, [ch 5, slip st in the last dc made (page 130)] 3 times, 5 dc in the next ch-3 sp, sc in the next sc; repeat from the * across.

Fasten off.

EDGING 3

Notes

This design uses 3 colors: Colors A, B, and C.

Single crochet 2 together (sc2tog) = [Insert the hook in the next st and pull up a loop] twice, yarn over the hook and draw it through all 3 loops on the hook.

Single crochet 3 together (sc3tog) = [Insert the hook in the next st and pull up a loop] 3 times, yarn over the hook and draw it through all 4 loops on the hook.

With Color A, chain a multiple of 8 + 2.

Row 1 (RS): Sc in the second ch from the hook and in each ch across, turn.

Row 2: Ch 1, sc in each sc across, turn.

Row 3: Ch 1, sc in the first sc, *hdc in the next sc, dc in the next sc, tr in the next sc, dtr in the next sc, tr in the next sc, dc in the next sc, hdc in the next sc, sc in the next sc; repeat from the * across, turn.

Row 4: Working in the back loop only, ch 1, sc2tog over the first 2 sts, *sc in each of the next 2 sts, 3 sc in the next st, sc in each of the next 2 sts, sc3tog over the next 3 sts; repeat from the * across, ending with sc in each of the next 2 sts, 3 sc in the next st, sc in each of the next 2 sts, sc2tog over the last 2 sts, turn. Change to Color B.

Rows 5 and 6: As Row 4. At the end of Row 6, change to Color C.

Rows 7 and 8: As Row 4.

Fasten off.

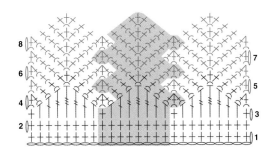

EDGING 4

Note

Picot = ch 3, slip st in the top/side of the last dc made (page 130).

Chain a multiple of 16 + 2.

Row 1 (RS): Sc in the second ch from the hook and in each ch across, turn.

Row 2: Ch 1, sc in the first sc, *ch 5, skip the next 3 sc, sc in the next sc, ch 3, skip the next 3 sc, 2 dc, ch 2, 2 dc] in the next sc, ch 3, skip the next 3 sc, sc in the next sc, ch 5, skip the next sc, ch 5, skip the next 3 sc, sc in the last sc; repeat from * across, turn.

Row 3: Ch 4 (counts as dc, ch 1 here and throughout), sc in the first ch-5 sp, *ch 3, skip the next ch-3 sp, dc in each of the next 2 dc, [2 dc, ch 2, 2 dc] in the next ch-2 sp, dc in each of the next 2 dc, ch 3, skip the next ch-3 sp, sc in the next ch-5 sp, ch 5, sc in the next ch-5 sp; repeat from * across, ending with ch 3, skip the next ch-3 sp, dc in each of the next 2 dc, [2 dc, ch 2, 2 dc] in the next ch-2 sp, dc in each of the next 2 dc, ch 3, skip the next ch-3 sp, sc in the next ch-5 sp, ch 1, dc in the last sc, turn.

Row 4: Ch 1, sc in the first dc, *ch 3, dc in each of the next 4 dc, [2 dc, ch 2, 2 dc] in the next ch-2 sp, dc in each of the next 4 dc, ch 3, skip the next ch-3 sp, sc in the next ch-5 sp; repeat from * across, ending with ch 3, dc in each of the next 4 dc, [2 dc, ch 2, 2 dc] in the next ch-2 sp, dc in each of the next 4 dc, ch 3, skip the next ch-3 sp, sc under the turning-ch-4, turn.

Row 5: Ch 1, sc in the first sc, ch 2, *dc in each of the next 6 dc, [2 dc, picot, 2 dc] in the next ch-2 sp, dc in each of the next 6 dc, ch 2, sc in the next ch-3 sp, ch 4, slip st in the third ch from the hook, ch 1, sc in the next ch-3 sp, ch 2; repeat from * across, ending with dc in each of the next 6 dc, [2 dc, picot, 2 dc] in the next ch-2 sp, dc in each of the next 6 dc, ch 2, sc in the last sc.

Fasten off.

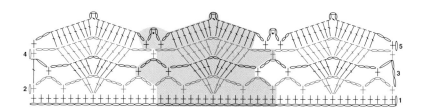

EDGING 5

Note

Double crochet 5 together (dc5tog) = Yarn over, insert the hook in next st and pull up a loop (3 loops are on your hook); yarn over and draw through 2 loops on the hook; [yarn over, insert hook in next st and pull up a loop; yarn over and draw it through 2 loops on the hook] 4 times, yarn over the hook and draw loop through all 6 loops on hook (page 123).

Picot = Ch 5, slip st in the top/side of the last sc made (page 130).

Chain a multiple of 10 + 2.

Row 1 (RS): Sc in the second ch from the hook and in each ch across, turn.

Row 2: Ch 5 (counts as dc, ch 2, skip the first 5 sc, *5 dc in the next sc, ch 2, skip the next 4 sc, dc in the next sc, ch 2, skip the next 4 sc; repeat from the *across, ending with 5 dc in the next sc, ch 2, skip the next 4 sc, dc in the last sc, turn.

Row 3: Ch 7, (counts as dc, ch 4), skip the first dc and ch-2 sp, *dc5tog over the next 5 dc, ch 4, dc in the next dc, ch 4; repeat from the * across, ending with dc5tog over the next 5 dc, ch 4, dc in the third ch of the turning-ch-5, turn.

Row 4: Ch 1, sc in the first dc, *4 sc in the next ch-4 sp, sc in the next dc5tog, 4 sc in the next ch-4 sp, sc in the next dc; repeat from the * across, ending with 4 sc in the next ch-4 sp, sc in the next dc5tog, 4 sc under the turning-ch, sc in the third ch of the turning-ch, turn.

Row 5: Ch 1, sc in first sc, picot, *sc in each of the next 5 sc, picot; repeat from the * across.

Fasten off.

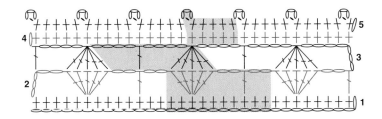

EDGING 6

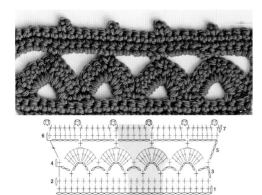

Note

Picot = Ch 5, slip st in the top/side of the last sc made (page 130).

Chain a multiple of 6 + 3.

Row 1 (RS): Sc in the second ch from the hook and in each ch across, turn.

Row 2: Ch 1, sc in each sc across, turn.

Row 3: Ch 4 (counts as hdc, ch 2), skip the first 2 sc, *sc in the next sc, ch 5, skip the next 2 sc, ch 3, skip the next 2 sc; repeat from the * across, ending with sc in the next sc, ch 5, sc in the next sc, ch 2, hdc in the last sc, turn.

Row 4: Ch 1, sc in the first hdc, *[5 dc, ch 1, 5 dc] in the next ch-5 sp, sc in the next ch-3 sp; repeat from the * across, ending with [5 dc, ch 1, 5 dc] in the next ch-5 sp, sc under the turning-ch-4, turn.

Row 5: Ch 9 (counts as tr, ch 5), skip the first sc, skip the next 5 dc, *sc in the next ch-1 sp, ch 5; repeat from the * across, ending with tr in the last sc, turn.

Row 6: Ch 1, sc in the first sc, *5 sc in the next ch-5 sp, sc in the next sc; repeat from the *across, ending with 5 sc under the turning-ch-9, sc in the fourth ch of the turning-ch-9, turn.

Row 7: Ch 1, sc in the first sc, *picot, sc in each of the next 6 sc; repeat from the * across, ending with picot.

Fasten off.

EDGING 7

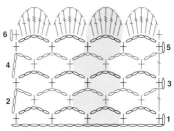

Chain a multiple of 5.

Row 1 (RS): Sc in the second ch from the hook, *ch 5, skip the next 3 ch, sc in each next ch; repeat from the * across, turn.

Row 2: Ch 5 (counts as dc, ch 2 here and throughout), sc in the first ch-5 sp, *ch 5, sc in the next ch-5 sp; repeat from the * across, ending with ch 2, dc in the last sc, turn.

Row 3: Ch 1, sc in the first sc, *ch 5, sc in the next ch-5 sp; repeat from the * across, turn.

Rows 4 and 5: As Rows 2 and 3, turn.

Row 6: Ch 1, sc in the first sc, *[hdc, dc, tr, dtr, tr, dc, hdc] in the next ch-5 sp; repeat from the * across, ending with sc in the last sc.

Fasten off.

EDGING 8

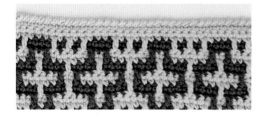

Notes

This design uses 2 colors: Colors A and B.

Always work in front of the ch-2 spaces of the previous 2 rows.

Carry the yarn loosely up the side after each stripe (page 139).

With Color A, chain a multiple of 8 + 4.

Row 1 (RS): Sc in the second ch from the hook and in each ch across, turn.

Row 2: Ch 1, sc in each sc across, turn. Change to Color B.

Row 3: Ch 1, sc in the first sc, ch 2, skip the next sc, *sc in the next sc, ch 2, skip the next sc, sc in each of the next 3 sc, ch 2, skip the next sc, sc in the next sc, ch 2, skip the next sc; repeat from the * across, ending with sc in the last sc, turn.

Row 4: Ch 1, sc in the first sc, ch 2, skip the next ch-2 sp, *sc in the next sc, ch 2, skip the next ch-2 sp, sc in each of the next 3 sts, ch 2, skip the next sc, sc in the next sc, ch 2, skip the next sc; repeat from the * across, ending with sc in the last sc, turn. Change to Color A.

Row 5: Ch 1, sc in the first sc, dc in the next skipped sc 3 rows below, *sc in the next sc, dc in the next skipped sc 3 rows below, ch 2, skip the next sc, sc in the next sc, ch 2, skip the next sc, dc in the next skipped sc 3 rows below, sc in the next sc, dc in the next skipped sc 3 rows below; repeat from the * across, ending with sc in the last 2 sc, turn.

Row 6: Ch 1, sc in each of the first 4 sts, *ch 2, skip the next ch-2 sp, sc in the next sc, ch 2, skip the next ch-2 sp, sc in each of the next 5 sts; repeat from the * across, ending with ch 2, skip the next ch-2 sp, sc in the next sc, ch 2, skip the next ch-2 sp, sc in each of the last 4 sts, turn. Change to Color B.

Row 7: Ch 1, sc in the first sc, ch 2, skip the next sc, *sc in each of the next 2 sc, dc in the next skipped sc 3 rows below, ch 2, skip the next sc, dc in the next skipped sc 3 rows below, sc in each of the next 2 sc, ch 2, skip the next sc; repeat from the * across, ending with sc in the last sc, turn.

Row 8: Ch 1, sc in the first sc, ch 2, skip the next ch-2 sp, *sc in each of the next 3 sts, ch 2, skip the next ch-2 sp; repeat from the * across, ending with sc in the last sc, turn. Change to Color A.

Row 9: Ch 1, sc in the first sc, dc in the next skipped sc 3 rows below, *ch 2, skip the next sc, sc in each of the next 2 sc, dc in the next skipped sc 3 rows below, sc in each of the next 2 sc, ch 2, skip the next sc, dc in the next skipped sc 3 rows below; repeat from the * across, ending with sc in the last sc, turn.

Row 10: Ch 1, sc in the first 2 sc, *ch 2, skip the next ch-2 sp, sc in each of the next 5 sts, ch 2, skip the next ch-2 sp, sc in the next st; repeat from the * across, ending with sc in the last sc, turn. Change to Color B.

Row 11: Ch 1, sc in the first sc, ch 2, skip the next sc, *dc in the next skipped sc 3 rows below, sc in each of the next 2 sc, ch 2, skip the next sc, sc in each of the next 2 sc, dc in the next skipped sc 3 rows below, ch 2, skip the next sc; repeat from the * across, ending with sc in the last sc, turn.

Row 12: Ch 1, sc in the first sc, ch 2, skip the next ch-2 sp, *sc in each of the next 3 sts, ch 2, skip the next ch-2 sp; repeat from the * across, ending with sc in the last sc, turn. Change to Color A.

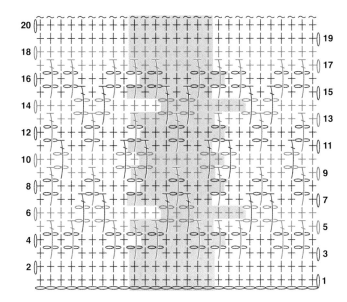

Row 13: Ch 1, sc in the first sc, dc in the next skipped sc 3 rows below, *sc in each of the next 2 sc, ch 2, skip the next sc, dc in the next skipped sc 3 rows below, ch 2, skip the next sc, sc in each of the next 2 sc, dc in the next skipped sc 3 rows below; repeat from the * across, ending with sc in the last sc, turn.

Row 14: Ch 1, sc in each of the first 4 sts, *ch 2, skip the next ch-2 sp, sc in the next st, ch 2, skip the next ch-2 sp, sc in each of the next 5 sts; repeat from the * across, ending with ch 2, skip the next ch-2 sp, sc in the next st, ch 2, skip the next ch-2 sp, sc in each of the last 4 sts, turn. Change to Color B.

Row 15: Ch 1, sc in the first sc, ch 2, skip the next sc, *sc in the next sc, ch 2, skip the next sc, dc in the next skipped sc 3 rows below, sc in the next sc, dc in the next skipped sc 3 rows below, ch 2, skip the next sc, sc in the next sc, ch 2, skip the next sc; repeat from the * across, ending with sc in the last sc, turn.

Row 16: Ch 1, sc in the first sc, ch 2, skip the next ch-2 sp, *sc in the next sc, ch 2, skip the next ch-2 sp, sc in each of the next 3 sts, ch 2, skip the next ch-2 sp, sc in the next sc, ch 2, skip the next ch-2 sp; repeat from the * across, ending with sc in the last sc, turn. Change to Color A.

Row 17: Ch 1, sc in the first sc, dc in the next skipped sc 3 rows below, *sc in the next sc, dc in the next skipped sc 3 rows below, sc in each of the next 3 sc, dc in the next skipped sc 3 rows below, sc in the next sc, dc in the next skipped sc 3 rows below; repeat from the * across, ending with sc in the last sc, turn.

Row 18: Ch 1, sc in each sc across, turn.

Row 19: As Row 18. Do not turn.

Row 20: Ch 1, working from left to right, reverse sc (page 131) in each sc across.

Fasten off.

EDGING 9

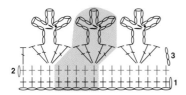

Chain a multiple of 5 + 3.

Row 1 (RS): Sc in the second ch from the hook and in each ch across, turn.

Row 2: Ch 1, sc in each sc across, turn.

Row 3: Ch 3 (counts as dc), skip the first 3 sc, *[2 dc, ch 8, slip st in the sixth ch from the hook, ch 5, slip st in the same ch as the last slip st) twice, ch 2, 2 dc] in the next sc, skip the next 4 sc; repeat from the * across, ending with [2 dc, ch 8, slip st in the sixth ch from the hook, 9ch 5, slip st in the same ch as the last slip st) twice, ch 2, 2 dc] in the next sc, skip the next 2 sc, dc in the last sc.

Fasten off.

EDGING 10

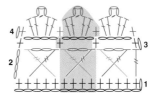

Note

Picot = Ch 3, slip st in the top/side of the last dc made (page 130).

Chain a multiple of 4 + 3.

Row 1 (RS): Sc in the second ch from the hook and in each ch across, turn.

Row 2: Ch 4 (counts as tr), skip the first 4 sc, *tr in the next sc, ch 2, working in front of the last tr made, tr in the first skipped sc; repeat from the * across, ending with tr in the last sc, turn.

Row 3: Ch 1, sc in the first tr, ch 4, skip the next tr, *ch 4, sc in between the next 2 tr; repeat from the * across, ending with ch 4, sc in the top of the turning-ch-4, turn.

Row 4: Ch 1, sc in the first sc, *[2 dc, picot, 2 dc] in the next ch-4 sp, sc in the next sc; repeat from the * across.

Fasten off.

EDGING 11

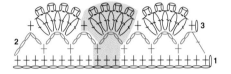

EDGING 12

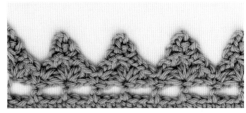

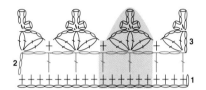

Notes

2-dc cluster = [Yarn over, insert hook in the indicated st and pull up a loop, yarn over and draw it through 2 loops] twice in same st, yarn over and draw it through all 3 loops on hook (page 119).

Picot = Ch 3, slip st in the top/side of the last 2-dc cluster made (page 130).

Chain a multiple of 6 + 5.

Row 1 (RS): Sc in the second ch from the hook and in each ch across, turn.

Row 2: Ch 4 (counts as dc, ch 1), skip the first 3 sc, *sc in the next sc, ch 5, skip the next 2 sc; repeat from the * across, ending with ch 2, dc in the last sc, turn.

Row 3: Ch 1, sc in the first dc, *[(2-dc cluster, picot) 4 times, 2-dc cluster] in the next ch-5 sp, sc in the next ch-5 sp; repeat from the * across.

Fasten off.

Note

2-dc cluster = Yarn over, insert the hook in the indicated st and pull up a loop, [yarn over and draw it through 2 loops] twice in same st, yarn over and draw it through all 3 loops on hook (page 119).

Chain a multiple of 6 + 2.

Row 1 (RS): Sc in the second ch from the hook and in each ch across, turn.

Row 2: Ch 5 (counts as dc, ch 2), skip the first 3 sc, *dc in the next sc, ch 2, skip the next 2 sc; repeat from the * across, ending with dc in the last sc, turn.

Row 3: Ch 3 (counts as dc), dc in the first dc, ch 5, slip st in the last dc made, ch 3, slip st in the last dc made, ch 3, sc in next dc *[(2-dc cluster, ch 3) twice, slip st in the last 2-dc cluster made, ch 5, slip st in the last 2-dc cluster made, ch 3, slip st in the last 2-dc cluster made, ch 3, 2-dc cluster] in the next st, sc in the next dc; repeat from the * across, ending with [2-dc cluster, ch 3] twice in the third ch of the turning-ch-5, slip st in the last 2-dc cluster made, ch 5, slip st in the last 2-dc cluster made.

Fasten off.

EDGING 13

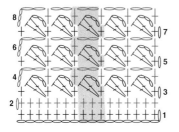

Chain a multiple of 3 + 2.

Row 1 (RS): Sc in the second ch from the hook and in each ch across, turn.

Row 2: Ch 1, sc in each sc across, turn.

Row 3: Ch 1, [sc, ch 3, 2 dc] in the first sc, skip next 2 sc, *[sc, ch 3, 2 dc] in the next sc, skip next 2 sc; repeat from the * across ending with sc in last sc, turn.

Row 4: Ch 5 (counts as dc, ch 2 here and throughout), skip the first sc, *sc in the next sc, ch 2; repeat from the * across, ending with sc in the third ch of the turning-ch-5, turn.

Row 5: Ch 1, [sc, ch 3, 2 dc] in the first sc, skip next 2 sc, *[sc, ch 3, 2 dc] in the next sc, skip next 2 sc; repeat from the * across ending with sc in third ch of turning ch-5, turn.

Row 6: As Row 4.

Rows 7 and 8: As Rows 5 and 6.

Fasten off.

EDGING 14

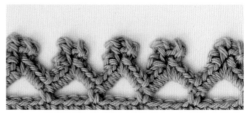

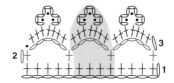

Note

Picot = Ch 3, slip st in the third ch from hook (page 130).

Chain a multiple of 4 + 2.

Row 1 (RS): Sc in the second ch from the hook and in each ch across, turn.

Row 2: Ch 1, sc in the first sc, *ch 5, skip the next 4 sc, sc in the next sc; repeat from the * across, turn.

Row 3: Ch 1, *[4 sc, 3 picots, 3 sc] in the next ch-5 sp; repeat from the * across, ending with a slip st in the last sc.

Fasten off.

EDGING 15

Chain a multiple of 8 + 6.

Row 1 (WS): Sc in the second ch from the hook, *[ch 3, skip the next ch, sc in the next ch] twice, ch 5, skip the next 3 ch, sc in the next sc; repeat from the * across, ending with [ch 3, skip the next ch, sc in the next ch] twice, turn.

Row 2: Ch 3 (counts as hdc, ch 1), sc in the next ch-3 sp, *ch 3, sc in the next ch-sp, ch 3, [sc, ch 3, sc] in the next ch-5 sp, ch 3, sc in the next ch-3 sp; repeat from the * across, ending with ch 3, sc in the next ch-sp, ch 1, hdc in the last sc, turn.

Row 3: Ch 3 (counts as dc), 2 dc in the first ch-1 sp, *ch 3, sc in the next ch-3 sp, ch 3, skip the next ch-3 sp, [2 dc, ch 1, 2 dc] in the next ch-3 sp, skip the next ch-3 sp; repeat from the * across, ending with ch 3, sc in the next ch-3 sp, ch 3, 3 dc under the turning-ch-3, turn.

Row 4: Ch 1, sc in the first dc, ch 5, slip st in the top/side of the last sc made (page 130), ch 3, slip st in the top/side of the last sc made, *ch 3, sc in the next sc, ch 3, sc in the next ch-1 sp, ch 3, slip st in the top/side of the last sc made, ch 5, slip st in the top/side of the last sc made, ch 3, slip st in the top/side of the last sc made; repeat from the * across, ending with ch 3, sc in the next sc, ch 3, sc in the top of the turning-ch-3, ch 3, slip st in the top/side of the last sc made, ch 5, slip st in the top/side of the last sc made.

Fasten off.

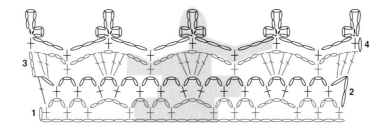

EDGING 16

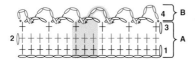

EDGING 17

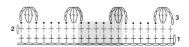

Note

This design uses 2 colors: Colors A and B.

With Color A, chain a multiple of 3 + 2.

Row 1 (RS): Sc in the second ch from the hook and in each ch across, turn.

Row 2: Ch 1, sc in each sc across, turn.

Row 3: Ch 1, sc in the first sc, *ch 3, skip the next 2 sc, sc in the next sc; repeat from the * across.

Fasten off Color A.

Row 4: With the RS facing, attach Color B with a slip st to the first sc, *ch 4, remove the loop from the hook, insert the hook under the next ch-3 of the previous row (see illustration), replace the loop onto the hook and pull it through the ch-3 sp of the previous row; repeat from the * across, ending with a slip st in the last sc.

Fasten off.

Note

3-dc cluster = [Yarn over, insert the hook in the indicated st and pull up a loop, yarn over and draw through 2 loops on the hook] 3 times in same st, yarn over and draw through all 4 loops on the hook (page 119).

Chain a multiple of 6 + 4.

Row 1 (RS): Sc in the second ch from the hook and in each ch across, turn.

Row 2: Ch 1, sc in each sc across, turn.

Row 3: Ch 3, skip the first sc, *3-dc cluster in the next sc, ch 3, slip st in each of the next 5 sc, ch 3; repeat from the * across, ending with 3-dc cluster in the next sc, ch 3, slip st in the last sc.

Fasten off.

EDGING 18

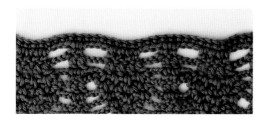

Note

Picot = Ch 3, slip st in the top/side of the last dc made (page 130).

Chain a multiple of 12 + 3.

Row 1 (RS): Dc in the fourth ch from the hook, *ch 4, skip the next 3 ch, dc in each of the next 4 ch, ch 4, skip the next 3 ch, dc in each of the next 2 ch; repeat from the * across, turn.

Row 2: Skip the first dc, dc in the next dc, *ch 3, [dc in the next dc, ch 1] 3 times, dc in the next dc, ch 3, dc in each of the next 2 dc; repeat from the * across, ending with ch 3, [dc in the next dc, ch 1] 3 times, dc in the next dc, ch 3, dc in the next dc, dc in the top of the turning-ch-3. turn.

Row 3: Ch 3 (counts as dc here and throughout), skip the first dc, dc in the next dc, *ch 3, sc in the next dc, [ch 3, sc in the next ch-1 sp] 3 times, ch 3, sc in the next dc, ch 3, dc in each of the next 2 dc; repeat from the * across, ending with ch 3, sc in the next

dc, [ch 3, sc in the next ch-1 sp] 3 times, ch 3, sc in the next dc, ch 3, dc in the next dc, dc in the top of the turning-ch-3, turn.

Row 4: Ch 3, skip the first dc, dc in the next dc, *ch 3, [sc in the next ch-3 sp, ch 3] 3 times, sc in the next ch-3 sp, ch 3, dc in each of the next 2 dc; repeat from the * across, ending with ch 3, [sc in the next ch-3 sp, ch 3] 3 times, sc in the next ch-3 sp, ch 3, dc in the next dc, dc in the top of the turning-ch-3, turn.

Row 5: Ch 3, skip the first dc, dc in the next dc, *ch 3, [sc in the next ch-3 sp, ch 3] twice, sc in the next ch-3 sp, ch 3, dc in each of the next 2 dc; repeat from the * across, ending with ch 3, [sc in the next ch-3 sp, ch 3] twice, sc in the next ch-3 sp, ch 3, dc in the next dc, dc in the top of the turning-ch-3, turn.

Row 6: Ch 1, sc in each of the first 2 dc, *ch 5, skip next ch-3 sp, sc in the next ch-3 sp, ch 2, dc in the next sc, picot, ch 2, sc in the next ch-3 sp, ch 5, skip next ch-3 sp, sc in each of the next 2 dc; repeat from the * across, ending with ch 5, skip next ch-3 sp, sc in the next ch-3 sp, ch 2, dc in the next sc, picot, ch 2, sc in the next ch-3 sp, ch 5, skip next ch-3 sp, sc in the next dc, sc in the top of the turning-ch-3.

Fasten off.

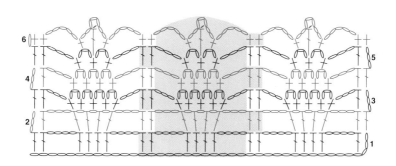

EDGING 19

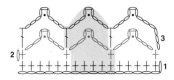

Note

Picot = Ch 3, slip st in the third ch from hook (page 130).

Chain a multiple of 5 + 2.

Row 1 (RS): Sc in the second ch from the hook and in each ch across, turn.

Row 2: Ch 1, sc in the first sc, *ch 3, picot, ch 3, skip the next 4 sc, sc in the next sc; repeat from the * across, turn.

Row 3: Ch 6 (counts as dc, ch 3), picot, ch 3, dc in the next sc, *ch 3, picot, ch 3, dc in next sc; repeat from the * across.

Fasten off.

EDGING 20

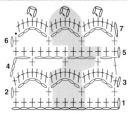

Note

Picot = Ch 3, slip st in the top/side of the last sc made (page 130).

Chain a multiple of 4 + 2.

Row 1 (RS): Sc in the second ch from the hook and in each ch across, turn.

Row 2: Ch 1, sc in the first sc, *ch 5, skip the next 3 sc, sc in the next sc; repeat from the * across, turn.

Row 3: Ch 1, sc in the first sc, *7 sc in the next ch-5 sp; repeat from the * across, ending with sc in the last sc, turn.

Row 4: Ch 4 (counts as dc, ch 1), skip the first 4 sc, *sc in the next sc, ch 3, skip the next 6 sc; repeat from the * across, ending with sc in the next sc, ch 1, skip next 3 sc, dc in the last sc, turn.

Row 5: Ch 1, sc in the first sc, sc in the next ch-1 sp, *sc in the next sc, 3 sc in the next ch-3 sp; repeat from the * across, ending with sc in the next sc, sc under the turning-ch-4, sc in the third ch of the turning-ch-4, turn.

Row 6: As Row 2, turn.

Row 7: Ch 1, *[4 sc, picot, 3 sc] in the next ch-5 sp; repeat from the * across, ending with a slip st in the last sc.

Fasten off.

EDGING 21

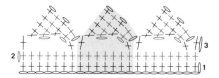

Chain a multiple of 7 + 2.

Row 1 (RS): Sc in the second ch from the hook and in each ch across, turn.

Row 2: Ch 1, sc in each sc across, turn.

Row 3: Ch 1, sc in the first sc, *ch 1, sc in the next sc, ch 1, turn; sc in the first sc, sc in next ch-1 sp, turn; ch 1, sc in the first sc, 2 sc in the next sc, turn; ch 1, 2 sc in the first sc, sc in each of the next 2 sc, turn; ch 1, sc in each of the first 3 sc, 2 sc in the next sc, skip next 5 sc in Row 2, sc in the next sc; repeat from the * across.

Fasten off.

EDGING 22

Chain a multiple of 10 + 2.

Row 1 (RS): Sc in the second ch from the hook and in each ch across, turn.

Row 2: Ch 1, sc in each sc across, turn.

Row 3: Ch 1, sc in the first sc, *hdc in the next sc, dc in the next sc, tr in the next sc, dtr in each of the next 3 sc, tr in the next sc, dc in the next sc, hdc in the next sc, sc in the next sc; repeat from the * across.

Fasten off.

EDGING 23

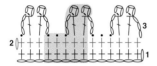

EDGING 24

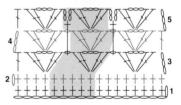

Note

Picot = Ch 3, slip st in the top/side of the last dc made (page 130).

Chain a multiple of 5.

Row 1 (RS): Sc in the second ch from the hook and in each ch across, turn.

Row 2: Ch 1, sc in each sc across, turn.

Row 3: Ch 3, skip the first sc, *[dc in the next sc, picot] twice, ch 3, slip st in each of the next 3 sc, ch 3; repeat from the * across, ending with [dc in the next sc, picot] twice, ch 3, slip st in the last sc.

Fasten off.

Chain a multiple of 5 + 3.

Row 1 (RS): Sc in the second ch from the hook and in each ch across, turn.

Row 2: Ch 1, sc in each sc across, turn.

Row 3: Ch 3 (counts as dc here and throughout), skip the first 3 sc, *[2 dc, ch 3, 2 dc] in the next sc, ch 1, skip the next 4 sc; repeat from the * across, ending with [2 dc, ch 3, 2 dc] in the next sc, skip the next 2 sc, dc in the last sc, turn.

Row 4: Ch 3, skip the first dc, *[2 dc, ch 3, 2 dc] in the next ch-3 sp, ch 1, skip the next ch-1 sp; repeat from the * across, ending with [2 dc, ch 3, 2 dc] in the next ch-3 sp, skip the next 2 dc, dc in the top of the turning-ch-3, turn.

Row 5: Ch 3, skip the first dc, *[2 dc, ch 3, 2 dc] in the next ch-3 sp, ch 2, sc in the next ch-1 sp 2 rows below, ch 2; repeat from the * across, ending with [2 dc, ch 3, 2 dc] in the next ch-3 sp, skip the next 2 dc, dc in the top of the turning-ch-3.

Fasten off.

RESOURCES

In this section, you'll find information about crochet instructions and charts, basic stitches, various techniques, and the crochet community—all you need to enjoy using this book.

ABBREVIATIONS

BPdc - back post double crochet stitch

BPtr - back post triple crochet stitch

ch(s) - chain(s)

ch-sp - chain space

dc - double crochet stitch

dc2tog - double crochet 2 together

dc3tog - double crochet 3 together

dc4tog - double crochet 4 together

dc5tog - double crochet 5 together

dtr - double triple crochet stitch

FPdc - front post double crochet stitch

FPdtr - front post double triple crochet stitch

FPst(s) - front post stitch(es)

FPtr - front post triple crochet stitch

hdc - half double crochet stitch

RS - right side

sc - single crochet stitch

sp(s) - space(s)

st(s) - stitch(es)

tr - triple crochet stitch

WS - wrong side

* - repeat instructions after asterisk or between asterisks across row or for as many times as instructed

[ ] - repeat instructions within parentheses for as many times as instructed

Note: American terms are used throughout this book. For UK equivalents, refer to the following chart below.

AMERICAN TERM	UK TERM
double crochet (dc)	treble crochet (tr)
double triple crochet (dtr)	triple treble crochet (tr tr)
gauge	tension
half double crochet (hdc)	half treble crochet (htr)
single crochet (sc)	double crochet (dc)
slip stitch	single crochet (sc)
triple crochet (tr)	double treble crochet (dtr)
yarn over	yarn over hook (YOH)

UNDERSTANDING INTERNATIONAL CROCHET SYMBOLS

In this section, discover how easy and fun it is to combine basic crochet stitches to create wonderfully textured fabrics. Here, post stitches, popcorns, and a few novelty maneuvers are used to stitch traditional ribbings, high-relief basketweaves, cables, and more.

COMPREHENSIVE GLOSSARY OF ALL SYMBOLS

⬭	chain	⊥	elongated single crochet (elongated sc)
•	slip stitch (sl st)	⊤̃	reverse sc (rev sc)
+	single crochet (sc)	⌡	long double crochet (long dc)
⊤	half-double crochet (hdc)	⌡	front post double crochet (FPdc)
⊤	double crochet (dc)	⌡	back post double crochet (BPdc)
⊤	treble crochet (tr)	⌡	front post triple crochet (FPtr)
⊤	double treble crochet (dtr)	⌡	front post double triple crochet (FPdtr)

single crochet 2 together (sc2tog)	3-triple crochet cluster (3-tr cluster)
single crochet 3 together (sc3tog)	perpendicular 2-dc cluster
double crochet 2 together (dc2tog)	long bobble
double crochet 3 together (dc3tog)	foundation row cluster/end of row cluster
double crochet 4 together (dc4tog)	main cluster
double crochet 5 together (dc5tog)	popcorn
triple crochet 2 together (tr2tog)	picot working sl st in the top/side of previous st
2-double crochet cluster (2-dc cluster)	picot working sl st in the third ch from hook
3-double crochet cluster (3-dc cluster)	worked in back loop only
4-double crochet cluster (4-dc cluster)	worked in front loop only
	marker

TIPS ON READING THE CROCHET CHARTS

The Foundation Chain is shown at the bottom of the picture, and each successive row is added from the bottom up, in the order they are crocheted. Rows are clearly numbered to help you keep track of your place in the pattern.

The picture always shows the fabric from the right side.

For patterns worked all in one color of yarn, right-side rows are shown in black and are read from right to left; wrong-side rows are shown in blue and are read from left to right.

The stitch repeat is shaded in gray.

The row repeat is indicated by a bracket on one side of the diagram.

For patterns that have more than one color, Color A is shown in purple; Color B in green; Color C in orange; and Color D in turquoise.

Some patterns have overlapping stitches. For clarity, stitches in front of others are outlined in white. Occasionally, gray or light blue indicates a stitch that is behind others.

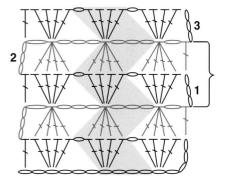

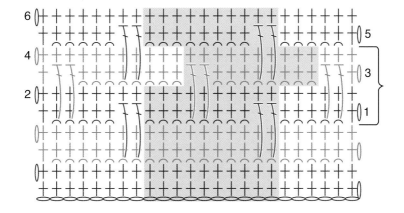

Resources: Understanding International Crochet Symbols

CROCHET TECHNIQUES

BASIC STITCHES

SLIP KNOT

Beginning at least 6" (15 cm) from the end of the yarn, make a loose loop, laying the loop on top of the yarn as it comes out of the ball. Use the crochet hook to grab the yarn, and tighten the loop to fit snuggly on the hook.

CHAIN (CH)

Place a slip knot on your hook. Yarn over and draw it through the loop on the hook to form the first chain. Repeat this step as many times as required. Note: In patterns, the loop on the hook is not included when counting the number of chain stitches.

1

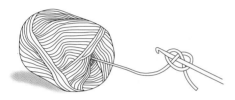

1

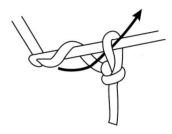

2

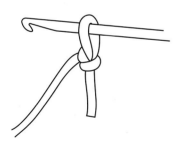

2

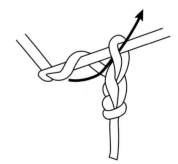

TURNING CHAINS

At the end of each row or round, a turning-chain is used to bring the hook and yarn to the height required for working the next row or round. A row of single crochet stitches, for example, has the same height as a single chain stitch, so before moving from one row of single crochet to another, you must chain one stitch to turn.

In all cases except single crochet, the turning-chain counts as the first stitch of the next row. After chaining three stitches to turn for a row of double crochet, for instance, you would insert your hook in the second stitch of the row; your last double crochet stitch would be worked in the top of the turning-chain-3 at the end of the row.

Refer to the following chart for recommended turning-chain heights:

Crochet Stitch	Corresponding Turning-Chain
Single crochet	Chain one
Half-double crochet	Chain two
Double crochet	Chain three
Triple crochet	Chain four
Double triple crochet	Chain five

SLIP STITCH (SL ST)

Insert the hook in the indicated stitch, yarn over and draw it through both the stitch and the loop on the hook.

1

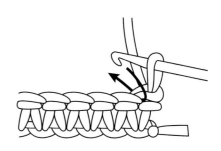

2

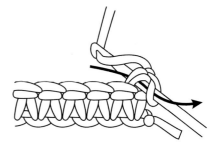

3

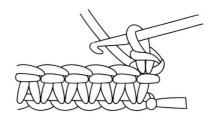

SINGLE CROCHET (SC)

Insert the hook in the indicated stitch, yarn over and pull up a loop (2 loops are on your hook); yarn over and draw it through both loops on the hook.

HALF-DOUBLE CROCHET (HDC)

Yarn over, insert the hook in the indicated stitch, yarn over and pull up a loop (3 loops are on your hook); yarn over and draw it through all 3 loops on the hook.

1

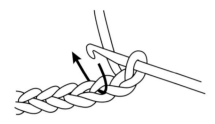

1

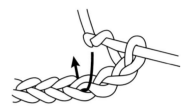

2

2

3

3

4

Essential Crochet Next-Level Stitches

DOUBLE CROCHET (DC)

Yarn over, insert the hook in the indicated stitch, yarn over and pull up a loop (3 loops are on your hook); [yarn over and draw it through 2 loops on the hook] twice.

TRIPLE CROCHET (TR)

[Yarn over] twice, insert the hook in the indicated stitch, yarn over and pull up a loop (4 loops are on your hook); [yarn over and draw it through 2 loops on the hook] 3 times.

1

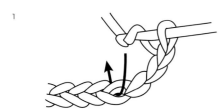

1

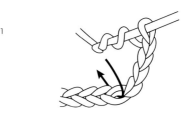

2

2

3

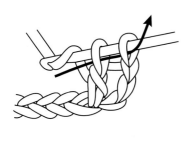

3

4

4

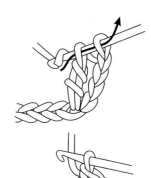

5

Resources: Crochet Techniques

DOUBLE TRIPLE CROCHET (DTR)

[Yarn over] 3 times, insert the hook in the indicated stitch and pull up a loop (5 loops are on your hook); [yarn over and draw it through 2 loops on the hook] 4 times.

1

2

3

4

5

6

Essential Crochet Next-Level Stitches

STITCH VARIATIONS

2-DC CLUSTER

[Yarn over, insert the hook in the indicated st and pull up a loop, yarn over and draw it through 2 loops] twice, yarn over and draw it through all 3 loops on hook.

3-DC CLUSTER

[Yarn over, insert the hook in the indicated st and pull up a loop, yarn over and draw it through 2 loops] 3 times, yarn over and draw it through all 4 loops on hook.

1

1

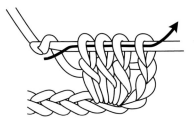

2

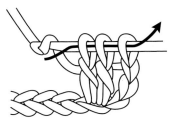

2

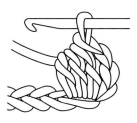

3

4-DC CLUSTER

[Yarn over, insert the hook in the indicated st and pull up a loop, yarn over and draw it through 2 loops] 4 times, yarn over and draw it through all 5 loops on hook.

5-DC POPCORN

Work 5 double crochet stitches in a stitch or space; drop the loop from the hook; reinsert the hook in the first double crochet stitch made, pick up the dropped loop and pull it through the first double crochet stitch.

1

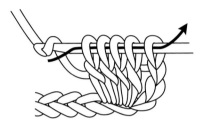

1

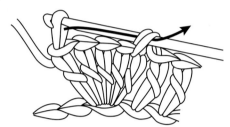

2

3-TR CLUSTER

[Yarn over] twice, insert the hook in the indicated st and pull up a loop, [yarn over and draw it through 2 loops on the hook] twice, yarn over and draw it through all 4 loops on the hook.

1

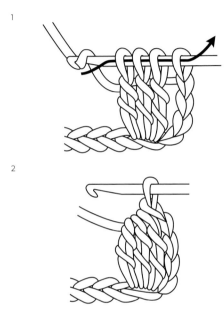

2

DOUBLE CROCHET 2 TOGETHER (DC2TOG)

Yarn over, insert the hook in the next st and pull up a loop; yarn over and draw yarn through 2 loops on hook, yarn over; insert the hook in the next designated st and pull up a loop, yarn over and draw yarn through 2 loops on hook, yarn over draw through 3 loops on hook.

1

2

DOUBLE CROCHET 3 TOGETHER (DC3TOG)

Yarn over, insert the hook in next st and pull up a loop (3 loops are on your hook); yarn over and draw through 2 loops on the hook; [yarn over, insert hook in next st and pull up a loop; yarn over and draw it through 2 loops on the hook] twice, yarn over and draw loop through all 4 loops on hook.

DOUBLE CROCHET 4 TOGETHER (DC4TOG)

Yarn over, insert the hook in next st and pull up a loop (3 loops are on your hook); yarn over and draw through 2 loops on the hook; [yarn over, insert hook in next st and pull up a loop; yarn over and draw it through 2 loops on the hook] 3 times, yarn over and draw loop through all 5 loops on hook.

1

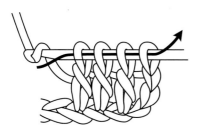

1

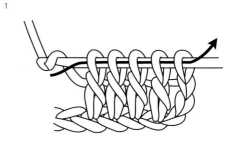

2

2

DOUBLE CROCHET
5 TOGETHER (DC5TOG)

Yarn over, insert the hook in next st and pull up a loop (3 loops are on your hook); yarn over and draw through 2 loops on the hook; [yarn over, insert hook in next st and pull up a loop; yarn over and draw it through 2 loops on the hook] 4 times, yarn over and draw loop through all 6 loops on hook.

1

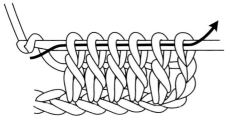

2

END OF ROW CLUSTER

[Yarn over and insert from front to back to front around the post of the dc 3 sts back, and pull up a loop (3 loops are on the hook), yarn over and draw it through 2 loops] 3 times (4 loops are on the hook), yarn over, insert the hook in the top of the turning-ch-3 and draw up a loop (6 loops are on the hook), yarn over, and draw it through 2 loops, yarn over and draw it through all 4 loops on hook.

1

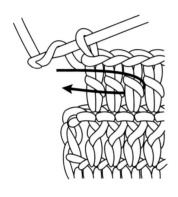

2

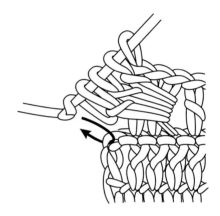

3

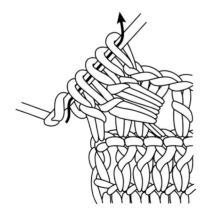

4

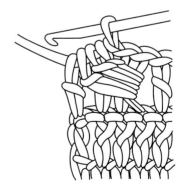

FOUNDATION ROW CLUSTER

[Yarn over and insert the hook from front to back to front around the post of the dc 3 sts back, and pull up a loop (3 loops are on the hook), yarn over and draw through 2 loops] 3 times (4 loops are on the hook), yarn over, insert the hook in the next ch and draw up a loop (6 loops are on the hook), yarn over, and draw through 2 loops, yarn over and draw it through all 5 loops on hook.

1

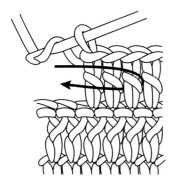

2

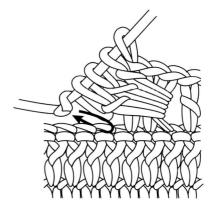

3

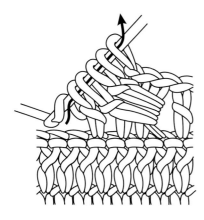

4

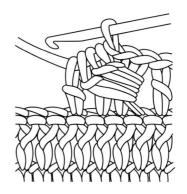

LONG BOBBLE

Yarn over, insert the hook around the post of next dc from front to back to front and pull up a loop, yarn over, and draw the hook through 2 loops on the hook, [yarn over, insert the hook from front to back to front around the post of same dc and pull up a loop, yarn over and draw the hook through 2 loops on hook] 3 times, yarn over and draw it through all 5 loops on hook.

1

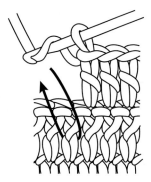

2

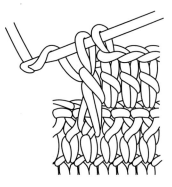

3

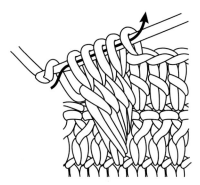

4

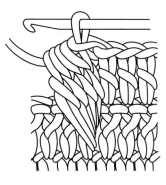

LONG DOUBLE CROCHET (LONG DC), WORKING OVER CHAIN SPACES IN ROWS BELOW

Make an elongated double crochet stitch worked in the next stitch the indicated number of rows below, pulling up the first loop until it is even with the hook.

1

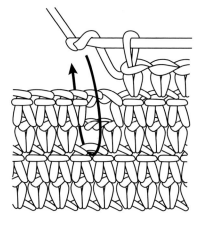

2

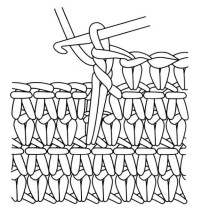

MAIN CLUSTER

[Yarn over and insert it from front to back to front around the post of the dc 3 sts back, and pull up a loop (3 loops are on the hook), yarn over and draw it through 2 loops] 3 times (4 loops are on the hook), [yarn over] twice, insert the hook from front to back to front around the post of the next FPst and draw up a loop (7 loops are on the hook), [yarn over and draw it through 2 loops] twice, yarn over and draw it through all 5 loops on hook.

1

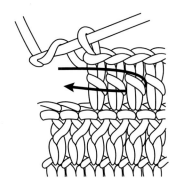

2

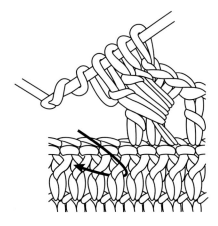

3

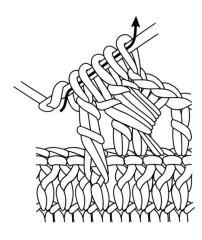

4

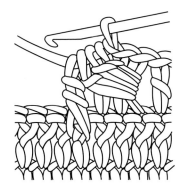

Essential Crochet Next-Level Stitches

PERPENDICULAR 2-DC CLUSTER

Yarn over, insert the hook through both the top of the last dc made as well as the side of the same dc and pull up a loop, yarn over and draw it through 2 loops] twice, yarn over and draw it through all 3 loops on hook.

1

2

3

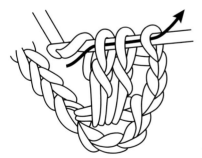

4

PICOT WORKING A SLIP STITCH IN THE TOP/SIDE OF LAST STITCH MADE

Working from the left to the right, insert the hook in the top and side (at once) of the last stitch made.

PICOT WORKING A SLIP STITCH IN THE THIRD CHAIN FROM HOOK

Ch 3, slip st in the third ch from the hook.

1

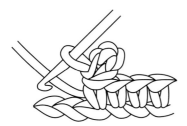

1

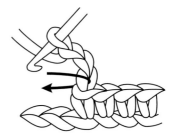

2

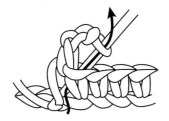

2

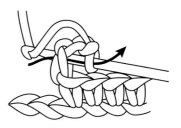

3

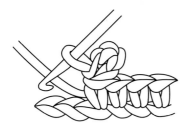

3

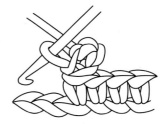

REVERSE SINGLE CROCHET

Working from left to right, insert hook in next stitch, yarn over and pull up a loop; yarn over and draw loop through both loops on hook.

1

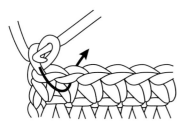

2

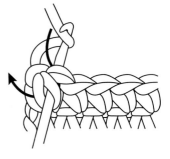

3

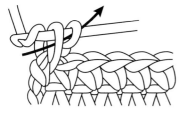

4

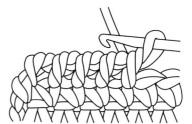

SINGLE CROCHET OVER PREVIOUS ROW(S)

To make a single crochet stitch over the last row, insert the hook at the base of the stitch one row below instead of into the top of it. Complete the stitch as an elongated single crochet stitch, working loose enough so that the stitch is the same height as the current row.

To make a single crochet stitch over the last two rows, insert the hook at the base of the stitch two rows below. Complete the stitch as an elongated single crochet stitch, working loose enough so that the stitch is the same height as the current row.

1

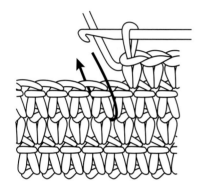

1

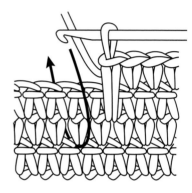

2

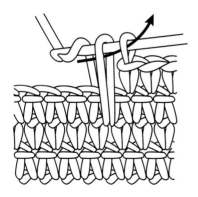

2

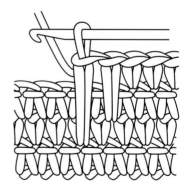

SINGLE CROCHET 2 TOGETHER (SC2TOG)

[Insert the hook in next stitch and draw up a loop] twice, yarn over and draw through all 3 loops on hook.

SINGLE CROCHET 3 TOGETHER (SC3TOG)

[Insert the hook in the next st and pull up a loop] 3 times, yarn over and draw through all 4 loops on hook.

1

1

2

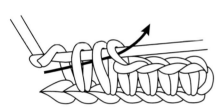

2

3

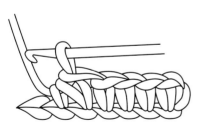

3

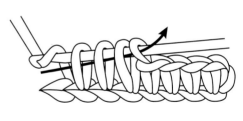

4

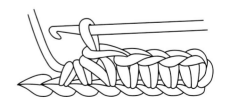

TRIPLE CROCHET 2 TOGETHER (TR2TOG)

*[Yarn over] twice, insert the hook in next indicated stitch, yarn over and pull up a loop, [yarn over and draw the hook through 2 loops on the hook] twice, repeat from * once, yarn over and draw it through all 3 loops on hook.

1

2

3

WORKING AROUND THE FRONT POST OF A STITCH

(as for Front Post Double Crochet (FPdc), Front Post Triple Crochet (FPtr) stitches or Front Post Double Triple Crochet (FPdtr) stitches)

Instead of working stitch in the top of the row below, insert the hook from front to back to front around the post of the indicated stitch in the row below as shown in the illustration, and complete the stitch the ordinary way.

1

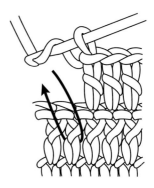

WORKING AROUND THE BACK POST OF A STITCH

(as for Back Post Double Crochet (BPdc) or Back Post Triple Crochet (BPtr) stitches)

Instead of working stitch in the top of the row below, insert the hook from back to front to back around the post of the indicated stitch in the row below as shown in the illustration, and complete the stitch the ordinary way.

1

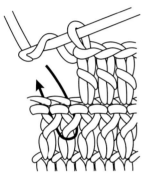

WORKING BEHIND THE LAST ROW

Keeping the last row to the front, work a stitch in the indicated stitch one or more rows below.

1

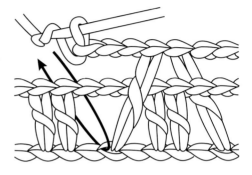

2

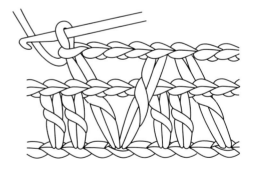

WORKING IN FRONT OF LAST ROW

Keeping the chain space of the previous row to the back of the fabric, work a stitch in the indicated stitch one or more rows below.

1

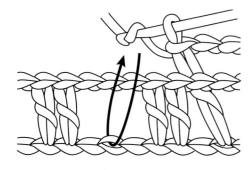

2

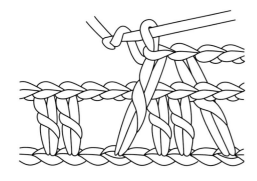

WORKING IN FRONT OF LAST TWO FRONT POST STITCHES

Yarn over as many times as is necessary for your desired stitch, then, working in front of the fabric, insert the hook from right to left and from front-to-back-to-front around the post of the first of the two skipped post stitches two rows below, and complete the front post stitch the regular way. Yarn over as many times as is necessary for your desired stitch, then, working in front of the fabric, insert the hook from right to left and from front-to-back-to-front around the post of the second of the two skipped post stitches two rows below, and complete the front post stitch the regular way.

1

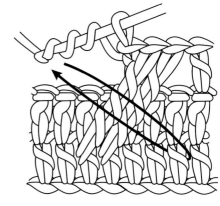

2

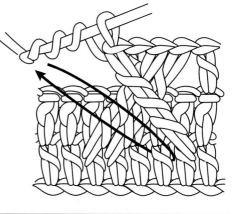

WORKING BEHIND LAST TWO FRONT POST STITCHES

Yarn over as many times as is necessary for your desired stitch, then, working in between the main fabric and the front post stitches just made, insert the hook from right to left and from front-to-back-to-front around the post of the first of the two skipped post stitches two rows below, and complete the front post stitch the regular way. Yarn over as many times as is necessary for your desired stitch, then, working in between the main fabric and the front post stitches just made, insert the hook from right to left and from front-to-back-to-front around the post of the second of the two skipped post stitches two rows below, and complete the front post stitch the regular way.

1

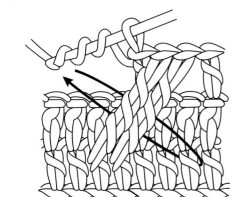

2

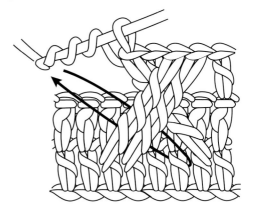

WORKING IN THE BACK OR FRONT LOOP ONLY

Rather than working in both loops of the indicated stitch, insert the hook under the back or front loop only, and complete the stitch the ordinary way.

1

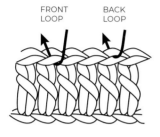

FRONT
LOOP

BACK
LOOP

WORKING INTO CHAIN SPACES

Rather than working in the individual chain stitches of the turning chain, insert the hook under the entire chain as a whole.

1

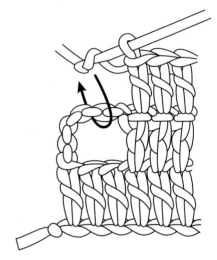

2

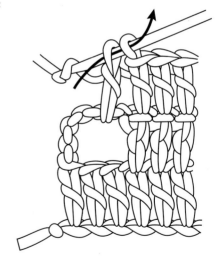

WORKING WITH COLOR

ATTACHING A NEW COLOR

Work the last stitch of the old color until two loops are on the hook, then, leaving a 6" (15 cm) tail, use the new color to complete the stitch.

1

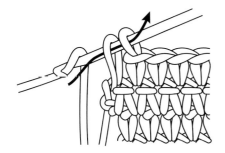

CARRYING THE YARN ALONG THE SIDE OF THE FABRIC

To minimize the number of yarn tails left to be darned in, yarns can be loosely carried up the edge of the fabric when working an even number of rows per stripe.

1

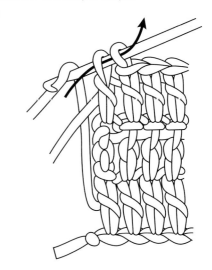

THE CROCHET COMMUNITY

To meet other crocheters and to learn more about the craft, contact the following organization:

THE CROCHET GUILD OF AMERICA

crochet.org

To meet other crocheters online, visit ravelry.com

Join my fan group on Ravelry to share photos of your projects and to keep up with my work. Go to ravelry.com/groups/melissa-leapman-rocks to be part of the fun!

ACKNOWLEDGMENTS

I am grateful to Jean, Shannon, Bob, Rob, Carly, and everyone at Cascade Yarn Company for sending me boxes (and boxes and boxes!) of beautiful yarn. Each swatch in this book was crocheted with Cascade 220, the perfect go-to wool yarn for great stitch definition and head-dizzying color choice. Thank you.

Special thanks go to Danelle Howard, my extraordinary project assistant for this book.

ABOUT THE AUTHOR

With over 1,450 designs in print, Melissa Leapman is one of the most widely published American crochet and knit designers working today.

As a freelance designer, she's worked with leading ready-to-wear design houses in New York City. Also, each season, top yarn companies commission Melissa to create designs promoting their new and existing yarns; her popular patterns and name recognition help them sell yarn.

Leapman is the best-selling author of many knitting and crocheting books. She has been a featured guest on numerous television shows, has hosted several Leisure Arts knitting and crocheting DVDs, and has written many crochet and knit leaflets for Leisure Arts and Annie's. Additionally, her designs are popular on web-based venues such as Mainly Crochet, Craftsy, and Ravelry.

Nationally, her workshops are popular with crafters of all levels. She teaches at every major knitting and crochet event, including STITCHES, VKLive, and the CGOA/TKGA shows, as well as at nearly every TNNA industry trade show for the past twelve years. Additionally, she has appeared at hundreds of yarn shops and local guild events across the country, working approximately twenty-five events every year, including one or two knit/crochet cruises.

To see more of her work, visit melissaleapman.com and @melissa.leapman on Instagram.

INDEX

Essential Crochet Next-Level Stitches